Christo Norden-Powers

Powerful Questions
That Highly Effective
Business Leaders Ask

to build successful, dynamic,
profitable organizations

Spandah

Published by Spandah Pty Ltd

A.B.N 23 104 743 393

www.spandah.com

The national Library of Australia Cataloging-in-Publication entry

Norden-Powers, Christo.

Powerful Questions that highly effective business leaders ask:
to build successful, dynamic, profitable organizations

Spandah 2010

ISBN 9780975818633 (pbk.)

1. Business - Decision making. 2. Problem solving.

3.Success in business. I. Title.

658.403

Previously published as:
Powerful Questions That Every Director, Executive & Manager Must Ask

Contents

For Edwina and Aimée
with love and gratitude.

What Clients say about *Powerful Questions* Workshops

"Asking the **Powerful Questions** is the best value that a Director can bring to a Board, ensuring that everyone is accountable and that the Directors are properly informed. The questions are ideal for identifying potential trouble spots. An excellent program. I apply the techniques constantly. It is a very useful process."

Leo Menkens, Director

"Great program, very insightful and a good use of time."

Graeme W. Horne, General Manager, AGL

"A powerful yet simple set of techniques that will enable me to ask relevant questions without appearing to question the integrity of others."

Vanessa Boully, Chairman, Royal Flying Doctor Service

"Excellent and clear structure that will provide great benefits to our Board."

John Fison, Director, Keltec Ltd (UK)

"This is an extremely practical workshop which can be applied immediately in every business situation."

Michael Wood, General Manager,
Kingston Property Constructions Pty Ltd.

"The **Powerful Questions** provide excellent essential skills for any Director or Executive in the public or private sector. The vital 'how to' skills."

Lindsay Oxlad, Director, Health Partners

"Useful in Board meetings, committees and difficult negotiations. The techniques will help in getting to the real situation. The **Powerful Questions** provide a very useful framework for getting to the facts. It's often what's not said that is more important than what is actually said."

Christine Hawkins, Director, Cinnabar International.

Author's note

Throughout this book I shall refer to using questions in conversations and discussions. The **Powerful Questions** are equally applicable to the written word and to the spoken word. Wherever I have referred to the conversations or discussions, the principle is the same for written documents, and vice versa.

There is, however, a different skill involved with hearing language patterns as opposed to reading them. You can read a document more than once to understand its meaning, whereas you will usually only hear the words in a conversation once and will generally have to phrase a question within a few seconds or minutes of hearing the relevant words before the words pass from memory.

You'll find exercises throughout the book that will assist to embed the skills – if you do the exercises! In the back of the book, you'll find some suggestions that will help you practice increasing your awareness and listening skills, and some resources that are available to fine-tune those skills.

What are *Powerful Questions*?

Powerful Questions are questions that are effective, incisive, high impact, challenging, useful, versatile and above all, simple. They are questions that shift consciousness and re-shape the mind, questions that cut to the core of thought processes and language.

The *Powerful Questions* are not simply questions about the facts and circumstances under enquiry. They work independently of the content of an interaction (the subject matter of discussion – the 'what') and activate the processes (the 'how') that underlie human communication and thinking. They give us the ability to dissect and re-create thinking and communication patterns using the perceptions, knowledge and experience of the person being questioned. They help people

- clarify their own thought processes and communication

- sort fact from fiction

- think from different perspectives

- take ownership, commitment and accountability.

The *Powerful Questions* are among the most useful in any business situation – at Board, executive, management and operational levels. It is, in fact, very useful to have people at *all* levels and functions of a business understand and become skilled with these techniques.

They are questions that:

- ✓ uncover what is not being said

- ✓ clarify meaning and intention

- ✓ focus on underlying motivation

- ✓ identify weaknesses in strategy and proposals

- ✓ create solutions and processes that work

- ✓ pinpoint issues

- ✓ identify the beliefs and perceptions behind conclusions and opinions

- ✓ cut through assumptions

- ✓ enable better and more effective choices, decisions and behaviours.

The **Powerful Questions** are the questions that people want to *avoid* when they want to pass blame and responsibility to others, to gain an advantage or to manipulate. They will save you and your business a lot of time, energy and money.

You don't have to know anything about the facts or circumstances being presented to you in order to ask these questions.

You simply have to be 'present' and listen. What the other person says will reflect their thinking processes, perceptions and beliefs. All the clues that you need are contained in the way that the other person expresses himself or herself. The questions enable you to elicit and understand the other person's reality, with crystal clarity.

They can be seamlessly integrated into a conversation or meeting, where they are hardly noticed, but nevertheless have significant influence on the direction and quality of the communication and decision processes.

They give you tremendous power to create useful outcomes in meetings, negotiations, coaching and mentoring scenarios, when mediating conflict and disputes, and when dealing with change.

These are the questions that highly effective business leaders ask, every day - whether they are Board members, executives, managers, supervisors or team leaders. Every truly effective leader in any field of endeavour understands that two of the greatest impediments to performance - especially in business - are the way we think and the way we communicate, both of which directly affect the success of an organisation, the energy, commitment and output of people in the organisation, and ultimately the profits of the organisation. The **Powerful Questions** provide you with an easy, quick way to *significantly* improve results in daily business interactions throughout the entire organisation and with clients, customers, business partners and other stakeholders.

The **Powerful Questions** are the single most effective (and cost-effective) way to improve your business, every day.

This book makes explicit

- the structure of the questions, and

- the process for knowing when and how to ask the questions

so that you can be in full command of the questions at any time and in any circumstances.

Spandah Pty Ltd
A.B.N 23 104 743 393
www.spandah.com
www.powerfulquestions.net
email: contactus@spandah.com

INTRODUCTION

The first years of this millennium earned the distinction of delivering some of the largest corporate collapses in history. It was a global phenomenon.

Enron, Parmalat, WorldCom and HIH are by-words in their respective countries (and globally) for executive greed, incompetence and poor governance. Together they resulted in many billions of dollars of losses to investors, suppliers, customers and employees.

A much wider community felt the 'ripple effect'. For instance, the collapse of HIH Insurance in Australia with $5 billion in debts almost stopped the home construction industry, for which HIH was a major underwriter. The flow-on to those who relied on home constructions for a living, the families of those people, and their communities, was well beyond the list of creditors that took HIH down.

In each case, the collapse was mainly, if not solely, due to choices made by the leaders of those companies. Many people and businesses were adversely affected by the actions and decisions of a handful of people.

Corporate disasters were substantially responsible for various changes to corporate governance laws and regulations that have since been implemented, such as Sarbanes-Oxley (USA) and Corporate Law Economic Reform Program legislation (known as CLERP 9) in Australia, and the changes to many Stock Exchange codes of practice and accounting codes around the world.

In some jurisdictions, the responsibilities and liabilities of the CEO and CFO have become more onerous, and governments are considering extending responsibilities and liabilities (including criminal liability) further down the organizations to senior and middle management levels.

Add to this picture the increasing expectations that investors have for standards of corporate governance and performance, together with the trend in courts towards imposing higher standards on corporate leaders, and we have a clearly changing landscape for business leaders - one that has some commentators concerned that business captains will be less willing to take the calculated risks that are essential to developing and growing a business, and less willing to take up executive or Board positions.

We have a clearly changing landscape for business leaders

The importance of asking questions

Post-Enron debate on corporate governance reforms led to reviews, worldwide, of corporate governance 'best practice'. One common outcome of those reviews was the need for corporate leaders to ask the questions that matter, described variously as the 'hard', 'tough' or 'right' questions. That is not surprising when you consider how often failing to ask the right questions – or any questions in some cases – contributes to the demise of even the most powerful and seemingly successful enterprises.

Failing to ask the right questions contributes to the demise of even the most powerful and seemingly successful enterprises.

Enron is a good example. Most debate about Enron focuses on the unethical activities of its leaders. But there was another factor that contributed to Enron's problems that eventually made it impossible for Enron to continue trading. In the days prior to its collapse, its executives were frantically attempting to arrange finance to enable it to continue to pay wages and other items. One of the executives asked: "What's our debt repayment schedule?" and was met with stunned silence. No one knew. "You mean we're a Fortune 500 company and we don't know how much we owe or when it's due?" asked another. Then one of the finance executives offered an explanation "No one's asked us before." After a quick phone around to tally Enron's debts, they knew that Enron would not survive.

Most finance executives would be amazed that the Enron executive team did not have its finger on the debt pulse. But the fact remains that they were so caught up in doing the big deals that they forgot the basics, and no one asked the questions.

It's not difficult to see why asking the right questions would be a key component of good governance. The right questions can identify potential problems, create solutions and generate opportunities that might otherwise not have been discovered.

On the other hand, not asking the right questions can quite easily cost medium and large companies millions, hundreds of millions, and even billions of dollars, and can easily cost small business tens

Not asking the right questions can quite easily cost companies millions of dollars.

of thousands or hundreds of thousands of dollars. Failing to ask the right questions can cost companies their reputation, corporate leaders their jobs, shareholders and business owners their investment.

The NAB

An example is the National Australia Bank. In 2003 the NAB's currency trading operations lost $360 million – approximately 10% of its profit - as a result of rogue trading activities at its forex desk. Once the loss became public, the bank's reputation took a beating in the media. Almost all of the Board members were replaced, as were many of the bank's senior executives, and the bank embarked on an expensive and extensive restructure and cultural change program.

A Business Sunday reporter asked Graeme Kraehe, the former Chairman of NAB, what he'd learned from the forex debacle. Mr Kraehe replied:

> *"...to not necessarily accept the information that is presented to you, be far more aggressive in questioning it."*

When asked how a director is supposed to get the right information, Mr Kraehe answered:

> *"With great difficulty...if there is not an openness in the relationship between the board and management it will be difficult for directors to fulfil their responsibilities."*

Cost of performance failure

One of the presenters at the 2004 World Economic Forum was the CEO of Bain & Co., a global consultancy. Bain & Co. estimated that fraudulent business leaders cost companies over US$300 billion worldwide in 2003.

But that paled in comparison to the cost of Board and executive 'performance failures', which Bain & Co. estimated worldwide at over $3 trillion during 2003.

A significant amount by any standards. It is around the value of all the real estate in Australia, lost in one year!

Unsolved problems and unexploited opportunities represent a huge hidden cost to business.

I have no doubt that the actual figure is, in fact, much higher if the performance failures below executive levels are also taken into account. There is not an organization, public or private sector, that does not have unresolved problems at all levels of the organization that are costing it money, time, morale and lost opportunity. In larger companies the cost is usually many millions of dollars. Unsolved problems and unexploited opportunities represent a huge hidden cost to business.

By asking the right questions most, if not all, of the facts underlying the assumptions can be identified and the problems resolved.

Losses caused by the failure to ask questions are a tragedy, because in most cases the questions only take a few seconds or a few minutes to ask and answer, but the losses can represent months or years of hard earned revenue or value.

Skills, culture, choices, leadership and values

Graeme Kraehe's answers highlight some important points.

1. Business leaders must be able to recognise when a question needs to be asked.

Business leaders at all levels of organizations are confronted daily with meetings, facts, opinions, assumptions, proposals, reports, problems and opportunities that require input or a decision from the leader. Most of the data they must consider is written in documents or is presented verbally in meetings or by telephone. Leaders must be able to recognise the thinking and language patterns that need to be verified, clarified or challenged. For instance, you might encounter those patterns in a meeting or negotiation when someone

- avoids giving details that may be open to criticism
- gives the appearance of encompassing all aspects or issues under discussion, but fails to identify the shortcomings of an action, strategy, solution or process.
- uses general language that does not answer the question or address the issue, but appears to do so
- uses specific language that does not answer the question or address the issue, but appears to do so
- phrases the answer to a question in a manner that suggests or implies X when in fact Y is the truth
- distorts data so that the data appears to have more validity than it in fact has

5

- omits details so that only part of the facts are conveyed

- is very specific on a certain aspect of the situation, distracting attention from another aspect of the issue that needs deeper consideration or questions

- appears to answer a question and then subtly shifts the topic or emphasis away from the question

- appears to know what they are talking about when in fact they know very little

- creates an impression that has no factual basis, or creates facts which imply something that is not true.

You'll undoubtedly recognize some of the patterns on that list. They are common in most organizations, and endemic in bureaucratic organizations where avoidance of accountability and commitment is an art form. We've probably all been on the receiving end of those patterns in our business and/or personal lives.

Many of us have used those patterns when they have suited us. They are commonly encountered in meetings, public relations, advertising, presentations, sales, negotiations, job applications, performance reviews – in fact, in most business circumstances.

The patterns can be used deliberately to deceive, manipulate, or perhaps as 'positive spin', but most of the time they are used with a relatively innocent motivation. More often than not, people are not consciously aware that they are using those patterns.

Either way, if you are the listener you are likely to be caught in the speaker's web unless you

✓ are aware of when those patterns are being used, and

✓ know which questions to ask to deal with the patterns.

Deliberate or unintentional?

Does it matter whether someone uses those patterns deliberately, with the intention to deceive, or unintentionally, perhaps not

6

realising what they are doing?

For instance,

- would it make a difference if someone who reported to you omitted some facts because they forgot them, or because they thought the facts were irrelevant; whereas the facts omitted were not only relevant, but critical to your being able to assess a serious risk to the business?

- would it be acceptable if your colleagues summarised or generalised their description of a potential strategy because that was the quickest way to convey the overall impression of the situation; whereas, unbeknown to your colleagues, the generalisation obscured the details that would have disclosed to you a potentially serious defect in the strategy under consideration?

- would it matter if a person presenting a proposal omitted certain details because they had not considered those details of the proposal; yet those details of the proposal were what would eventually make or break its success?

Perhaps you might be tougher on someone who was deliberately deceptive compared to someone who innocently omitted important information, but from the point of view of the business, it makes no difference. The risk or loss is the same either way. Business leaders must be able to recognise the patterns that may cause problems and must know the questions that work for those patterns.

Listening at the speed of conversation

It is not always easy to identify potential issues while you are attempting to understand the content of a conversation that is moving at 200 words a minute.

It is also not easy to notice the subtleties of language that hide issues in reports and proposals when you are pressed for time.

We often see this at our *Powerful Questions* Workshops. Delegates are asked to bring an actual report or proposal relating to their business. They deliver the report or proposal to other delegates at the workshop (who act as their 'Board'). The 'Board' then asks the questions, often without knowing anything about the background to the issues or facts in the report.

•   After being questioned by his 'Board' at the workshop a well-respected and very experienced Chairman of a Top 500 company commented that he'd missed 75% of the issues in a report that had been presented to his actual Board some months earlier.

- An Executive of a company was questioned about a report that he provided to his 'Board' at a *Powerful Questions* workshop. In minutes the workshop delegates uncovered an issue that had caused the company to lose $4.5 million. That loss could have been avoided had the right questions been asked several months earlier by his executive team.

- A CEO commented that if his real Board had asked him the questions that the workshop delegates had asked, his Board would never have approved his proposal.
His comment: "I got away with it".

The Chairman, Executive and the real Board in those instances were not aware that
- ➢ potential risks were buried in the reports

- ➢ the reports contained language clues that pointed to potential risks

- ➢ they could have asked some simple questions to expose those risks.

Instead, they had been focused on the content of the reports.

The reports had been crafted and written to sound good, to sound like everything was in its place, but to the initiated ear the way that the language was used gave clues about risk and 'spin' that was missed at the original meetings.

8

What you don't learn at business school

But then, who can blame the Board? Business schools rarely provide courses on how to listen and question at the skill level required by business leaders, who are expected to acquire questioning skills by experience.

The problem is, of course, that the shareholders, courts and markets are unforgiving, and expect business leaders to have developed those skills.

Focus on the process

You do not need to know any background on the issues to be able to ask the right questions. That may seem like a strange assertion, but it is true. That's not to say that some background information and knowledge is not helpful – it generally is useful and will often shorten discussions. But background information is content-based. The **Powerful Questions** are not based on the *content* of what is said, but on the *process* underlying the language.

If you are attuned to the process, you can elicit any content that you need in order to understand and deal with the issues that may lurk in the report, proposal or discussion.

Deep hearing skill

The skill of knowing when to ask questions is a skill that can be learned. It is a listening skill, a state of awareness. It is, in particular, a deep hearing skill*.

The skill of knowing when to ask questions is a deep hearing skill.

By that I mean that you must be able to hear beyond the obvious words and meaning, and notice the shifts of direction, intention and focus behind the words, and the impact that the words have

---

*Techniques to develop this state of awareness are available on the CD 'Powerful Awareness - deep hearing states' at www.spandah.com or www.amazon.com

on your awareness. In particular, to be aware when something is missing from the information, when information is distorted or when the language indicates that the speaker's thought process may be self-limiting.

When those warning bells are heard, you know that it is time to probe deeper.

When those warning bells are heard, you know that it is time to probe deeper and to verify the facts, opinions and assumptions that are being expressed, or to test or shift the speaker's thought process.

2. Business leaders must have excellent questioning skills

The questions that leaders use fall under three broad categories:

➢ questions that reveal the facts

➢ questions that develop strategies, solutions and opportunities

➢ questions that empower people and the organization to perform at their best.

Graeme Kraehe's comments relate to questions that reveal the facts, potential problems and risks. But once the facts are ascertained the key to progressing any situation is found in the second point – questions that develop strategies, solutions and opportunities – and then in the third point, performance.

Questions that reveal facts

Organizations spend a lot of time and resources developing decision-making skills of their leaders and potential leaders. However, having good quality data is a prerequisite to making a quality decision.

Leaders are generally several steps removed from the source of information, the raw data. They often do not have direct knowledge of the facts, and primarily rely on others to provide the facts.

Quality data is a prerequisite to making a quality decision.

Therein lies the risk - a huge risk that is not addressed by the risk management protocols in many companies. If the organization's leaders are to make informed decisions and exercise good business judgment they need to have good quality, reliable data on which to base their decisions. If the data is faulty, the decision is more likely to be faulty.

By the time the data reaches the decision-makers, it has often passed through the hands of various people, and could have been distorted at a number of points along its journey from raw fact to presentation.

All data, whether presented as fact or opinion, risks being corrupted (usually unintentionally) at various stages as it is processed by the human mind, depending on:

- how accurately we perceive a fact (e.g. what we saw or heard)
- the meaning we attribute to a fact (e.g. "The clients responded negatively")
- how we process the meaning (e.g. "We're wasting time pursuing that client")
- how accurately we memorise the fact
- how accurately we recall the fact
- how accurately we describe the fact or meaning to someone else
- how accurately the other person perceives (hears) what we describe.

And so the cycle continues with the next person.

At each of those stages we make choices that are not necessarily based on fact, but are based on a far flimsier foundation - personal reality.

Gary Zukav demonstrated the difficulties associated with personal reality in his book *The Dancing Wu Li Masters*:

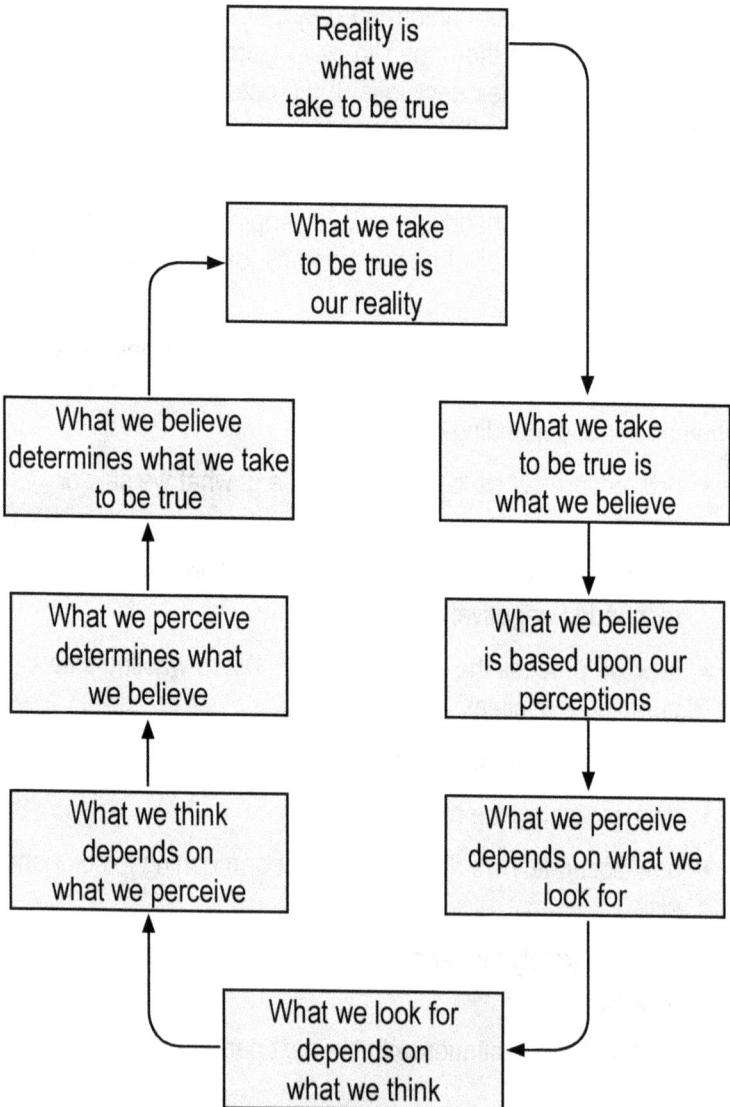

```
                    ┌─────────────────┐
                    │   Reality is    │
                    │    what we      │────────┐
                    │ take to be true │        │
                    └─────────────────┘        │
                                               │
           ┌─────────────────┐                 │
           │  What we take   │                 │
      ┌───▶│  to be true is  │                 │
      │    │   our reality   │                 │
      │    └─────────────────┘                 │
      │                                        ▼
┌──────────────────┐              ┌──────────────────┐
│ What we believe  │              │  What we take    │
│determines what we take          │  to be true is   │
│   to be true     │              │ what we believe  │
└──────────────────┘              └──────────────────┘
      ▲                                    │
      │                                    ▼
┌──────────────────┐              ┌──────────────────┐
│ What we perceive │              │ What we believe  │
│ determines what  │              │ is based upon our│
│   we believe     │              │   perceptions    │
└──────────────────┘              └──────────────────┘
      ▲                                    │
      │                                    ▼
┌──────────────────┐              ┌──────────────────┐
│  What we think   │              │ What we perceive │
│   depends on     │              │depends on what we│
│ what we perceive │              │     look for     │
└──────────────────┘              └──────────────────┘
      ▲                                    │
      │    ┌──────────────────┐            │
      └────│ What we look for │◀───────────┘
           │   depends on     │
           │  what we think   │
           └──────────────────┘
```

It is crucial for leaders to be able to sort through personal reality, interpretations, assumptions, guesses, beliefs and opinions as well as the blame, self-justification and excuses and other avoidance patterns that people use, and get to the facts.

Questions that develop solutions, strategies and opportunities

Once you have uncovered the facts of the situation, you are in a stronger position to make decisions, and develop solutions, strategies and opportunities to rectify any problem that is exposed by the facts, or to exploit any opportunity arising from the facts.

There are two primary styles used by leaders when it comes to developing solutions, strategies and opportunities

- telling their people the answers
- empowering their people to develop the answers.

The first style tends to limit possibilities to the output of one mind (the leader's mind), whereas the second style tends to open up possibilities by tapping into a broader consciousness and varied experience. That is a powerful skill for any leader, because it enables you to leverage the knowledge in your organization well beyond the sum of its parts. Questions form a large part of that skill. The questions in this book are designed for the empowering leadership style.

Questions that empower people and the organization to perform at their best

Asking questions can be an extraordinarily powerful and effective way to create engagement and commitment in business. In fact, questions are by far the easiest way to achieve those outcomes.

Consider your own experience. Is your commitment and ownership of a solution or strategy higher when you are told what to do, or when you are asked to help figure out how to do it?

The *Powerful Questions* can be used to empower people, and some empowering applications will be covered in this book.

However, the full extent to which these questions can be used to empower, and the various techniques for doing so, are dealt with comprehensively in **The Master Process**, workshops.

Why are more questions not asked?

Many business leaders do not recognise the patterns of language that indicate a potential problem. Or, if they do recognise the patterns, it is generally a 'gut feel' that is not crystallised and is quickly replaced by more tangible issues. As a result, in most instances, they will let the matter go, and not probe further.

There are several other reasons commonly given for making a conscious choice to refrain from asking questions in the business environment.

Don't know enough about the subject matter

One of the reasons given by directors, executives and managers for not asking a question or a follow-up question, despite their misgivings about the proposal or information, is that they do not have enough knowledge of the subject matter to be able to craft a useful question.

That need not be a concern with the **Powerful Questions**. You don't need to know a lot about the subject to ask the questions.

You don't need to know a lot about the subject to ask the questions. The effect of being able to do that is quite liberating.

It is possible to ask insightful questions that deliver excellent results simply by understanding how the speaker is structuring their language and how that structure reflects the speaker's thinking, even if you do not fully understand the content of the discussion. The effect of being able to do that is quite liberating.

As one director put it:

"I'm no longer overwhelmed by the data, proposals and arguments put forward by my colleagues on the Board. There's no need for

me to sit back and let them make decisions on matters that are not in my area of expertise.

I can hear the weaknesses in what is proposed by listening to the shifts in language patterns, and I am able to ask the questions that identify the real issues and then move to solutions. The first time I did that, I received several emails from my co-directors after the meeting stating that it was the best, most informative meeting we'd had."

That skill enables you to deal effectively with virtually any matter, even if you have no background knowledge or technical expertise. The person who provides the report, proposal or presentation under consideration, or who is asserting a fact or opinion, will (or ought to) have the knowledge and expertise to support their contention.

With the right questions you can elicit the necessary information, verify it, challenge it and improve it by drawing on their knowledge, as well as by adding in your own knowledge. If they can't provide the required information then you'll know that there may be a risk in relying on their assertions unless you can obtain the information from another source.

Even if you know nothing about the subject matter, the shifts in the other person's language will often point to a potential problem, and a few simple questions may be all that is necessary.

For instance as we'll see later on, one of the common shifts in language that indicates a potential risk or problem is the shift from specific to global language. If you recognise that pattern, any potential risk can usually be identified with two or three questions.

Case Study:

Some years ago I was asked to assist an insurer on an insurance claim that involved fuel contamination. I read the scientist's report that alleged that a delivery of fuel had been contaminated by a foreign substance during transit. The story was plausible because the freight company used the same tankers to transport a different cargo (the alleged contaminant) from time to time.

I knew nothing about fuel contamination and had only a high school knowledge of the chemistry involved in the case, but what I noticed was a shift in the quality of description in the scientist's report. The language was quite specific in its analysis of the history, test procedures and chemistry associated with the problem, but the language shifted from specific descriptions to a global description for one phrase in the middle of the report. That indicated to me that there was a high probability that something was not being reported accurately – the insurer was being given some 'spin' on the facts.

I called a specialist at the local university, faxed the report to him and in minutes he identified the flaw in the report and analysis methodology that showed that the insurer was being conned. A slight shift in language pattern saved the client $500,000 in claims.

Silly questions

Another commonly stated reason for not asking a question is that colleagues may think it's a silly question. This is a phenomenon that occurs at all levels of organizations. I hear it at Board, executive and management levels.

It is an unhelpful response that arises from wanting to be right, wanting to be respected and not wanting to look stupid.

I heard something similar from my 10-year-old daughter, Aimée, last year. The teacher had written a note on her schoolwork that concerned her. I asked what the note meant and it soon became clear that Aimée was not asking questions about the maths processes that she did not fully understand. She said that the other kids would think she's stupid for not knowing how to do the calculations.

The next morning we both talked to the teacher. I simply said: *"Can you please tell Aimée how many kids in the class actually understand how to do these calculations?"*

The teacher replied *"About 40%."*

I asked *"How many kids at this age don't ask you questions about how to do the maths because they are afraid of what other kids may think about them?"*

Answer *"Most, which is unfortunate because they take longer to learn and it makes my job harder. Dealing with that is part of growing up."*

"So," I asked, *"if Aimée were to take the lead and ask the questions, she'd not only be learning quicker, she'd also be helping 60% of the other kids to learn?"*

A smile came onto Aimée's face.

That afternoon when Aimée came home from school, she was very pleased with herself. She'd asked questions, learned how to do the calculations that she had thought were difficult, and some of her friends had commented that they were pleased that she'd asked because they also hadn't understood the maths.

Her confidence increased, along with her results, and she learned a little about what it takes to be a leader.

> **There is no such thing as a silly question.**
> **If you need to know, you need to know.**

If you do not understand what is said, or how a proposal will work, or what the implications are, then ask.

It takes courage to ask some questions, but the rewards can be significant. I read an article recently about a young, upwardly **If you do not understand, then ask.** mobile manager in a large bureaucratic organization. He'd had great success at improving a large division in the company. The headline screamed: "*I love asking stupid questions*".

He asked the questions that no one else had dared to ask for many years such as "*Why are we doing it this way?*" and, even better: "*Why are we doing this at all?*"

His division is an 'assumption-free zone', and one of the best performing divisions in the business.

Leaders are found at every level of any organization, if you look hard enough. The obvious candidates are Board members, executives and managers. I also include supervisors and team leaders in the definition for the purposes of asking questions. In reality, anyone can be a leader in any particular situation.

Effective leaders

- help others find the way forward

- ask the questions that elicit the facts, the truth, the processes that work, so that they can improve their knowledge and make the best decisions

- encourage others to challenge them, to ask them the tough questions

- answer the tough questions

- understand that they should obtain the best available information possible so as to make an informed decision and take the right action

- ask questions about something that doesn't make sense, or might not work, rather than be concerned that someone else may think the question is irrelevant, or the answer obvious

- know that if they don't have the correct information, the chances are much higher that they will make a wrong decision or wrong choice of action – a decision or action that does not work and that costs them or their business time and money.

Once you start asking questions, you'll often find that other people in a meeting will take up the issue and continue the questions. It is quite common for the initial questions to open up discussion on elements of the issue that no one had thought about, until you asked the question. Others who may have assumed a certain meaning to the language will pick up on details of the answers to your questions.

A new director related her experience to me:

"I hadn't been on a Board before, and I found a large part of the meetings a bit difficult to understand. When I started to ask the questions, several other long-term directors then added further questions that arose from their experience, and which I hadn't thought of. It appears that the more experienced directors assumed they knew what things meant, until I asked the dumb questions, and then they could see implications that I was not aware of, and they wanted to know more about the issue. Now I realise that, even if the topic is outside my experience, I can ask questions that are useful. The result is that I am enjoying the meetings more because I understand more and feel in control."

Others taking offence

Sometimes we may feel that asking the challenging questions may cause umbrage to colleagues, bosses or those who report to us, who may think that we don't trust them or their judgement, or who may act defensively to being asked questions.

The best business leaders actually prefer to be challenged by their colleagues. Perhaps the most difficult choice is to ask your boss the hard questions. However, in my experience, the best business leaders actually prefer to be challenged by their colleagues. The challenging questions hone their thinking, identify potential pitfalls that they may not have predicted and provide greater opportunity to think outside their normal patterns and experience.

Some years ago one of my friends, Greg, attended a departmental briefing in his organization with a couple of hundred other middle managers. The executive who was conducting the briefing clearly had a different perception of the facts compared to everyone else in the room but the audience said nothing because they weren't prepared to rock the boat. Greg asked a few questions of the executive and then stated: "I don't know where you get your information, but in my view it is quite wrong", and then proceeded to spell out the facts from his frontline experience. The executive asked his name. A month later, Greg was promoted to head office, reporting directly to the executive, who told Greg that he was tired of sycophants who didn't tell him the facts - they actually made his job harder to do well.

Executive coaches are familiar with the need to 'tell it as it is'. When I coach executives and directors, there inevitably comes a time when I have to challenge them to step beyond their comfort zone and to face some of the challenges of being all that they know they can be. It's often tough for them to do, but that's why they engage a coach to stretch them. When they make the breakthrough they have no regrets.

Backing off from asking questions because someone may not like the questions is not a good excuse, and does not serve the company, or you, or the other person. In a business environment it's better, in my view, to ask the hard questions and deal with the response; and to create a culture where asking questions is supported.

Here are some useful guidelines:

> - **Proactively question what is put before you**
> - **Take responsibility for challenging and probing**
> - **Do not assume that the information is fair, accurate or unbiased**
> - **Spend the time necessary to get the facts right**
> - **Engage, and give time for, open, frank discussions and meaningful debate**
> - **Learn how to ask incisive questions before you have to.**

One comment on the third point: it does not mean that you should assume that the information is unfair, inaccurate or biased. It simply means that if the information is important, test it to ensure that you are getting accurate, balanced data.

How to ask the challenging questions

How you ask a question, and your intention when asking, will count a great deal towards how the question is received. The questions in this book are often challenging to the recipient, and are best delivered conversationally, with a 'silk laser' - focused, and relaxed, so that the question is hardly noticed but, if necessary, asked with persistence.

An aggressive approach is usually not necessary and is generally counter-productive in a business environment, causing people on the receiving end of the questions to resist answering, to be defensive or less cooperative, or to take offence, resulting in a loss of rapport. When I shifted career from trial lawyer to corporate consultant I had to learn how to ask questions differently. I found that I could achieve much more by respecting the person to whom I addressed the questions, no matter what the circumstances. I was not there to judge them, or to embarrass them about their failures, but to help them achieve a business outcome that worked for them. By the same token, my job was to ensure that the right questions were asked, even if they caused some discomfort.

My intention when asking the questions was a key factor in making that transition. This is the key:

The over-riding attitude and intention that works for the Powerful Questions:

Ask the questions to;
clarify,
find the facts,
understand,
empower,
improve the situation,
and
to find out what will work best.

There is no element of blame, self-justification, disparagement, denigration, put-down, or 'right -vs.- wrong' in that approach. The questioner's ego is left at the door, as the saying goes.

Ensure that the question is answered

There are three critical competencies necessary for effective questioning skills:

- knowing when a question needs to be asked

- asking the right question and

- ensuring that the question is answered.

Even if we do ask the right question, many, many times we simply do not recognize when the answer does not accurately address the question.

The answer may sound good, but does not provide the information requested. It is, in fact, very common that the question is not answered fully or accurately and that neither party realises it.

When the questioner's mind engages the answer, it follows the language of the answer quite naturally in the direction nominated by the person answering.

Short answers are less of a problem, but once an answer goes beyond the first phrase or sentence, the answer will generally develop into an explanation, excuse, justification, reason, historical dissertation or future projection which, if executed smoothly, will slide your mind away from the point of the question, seamlessly re-directing and re-focusing it to where the speaker chooses to lead you.

Listen to a politician being interviewed when they or their party are under criticism and you'll experience that phenomenon. A few good interviewers are alert to the tactic, but most will miss the diversion in the answer.

After asking a question it is essential that you listen for whether the question you asked has been answered. You'll usually know within the first few moments of the answer.

For example:

Q: What are you doing that's not working?

A: Well, what's not working is the sales initiative. We're not getting anywhere near our sales target.

The first four words in that answer would alert you to the likelihood that the question is not going to be answered. What the person has answered is a different question:

What's not working?

That is a less focused question, whereas what the original question asked for was information about what the person is doing that's not working - in other words, behaviours that aren't working. If the discussion follows the answer, it is likely to focus on the sales initiative and sales targets, not the behaviour that led to the sales targets being missed.

Notice that the answer contained non-specific, global language – 'sales initiative', 'not getting anywhere near', 'sales target' - that is, typically, language that is used when a person is consciously or unconsciously avoiding responsibility. The question "What are you doing that's not working?" was directed towards personal responsibility and, if answered, would require specific behavioural descriptions.

When the question requires a specific response and the answer is non-specific, you can be fairly certain that you'll get the 'run around' unless you repeat the question. It is very important that the question is answered, because if the answer is off track, everything else moves with it – off track. If the question is not answered, ask it again.

There is a simple art to repeating the question. When you repeat the question, simply emphasise the word that you want the person to focus on, and you will re-direct their awareness to the key issue:

*Yes, but what are you **actually doing** that isn't working?*

That question ought to produce a much more useful answer, which can then be turned quite easily into a better strategy for your desired outcome by asking questions that empower, improve, discover what will work best and that focus accountability,
e.g.: *So, how can you do it in a way that **will** work?*

The questions have to be asked

There is, in fact, no good reason why challenging questions should not be asked. You may have to consider the timing and phrasing of the question for cultural reasons or to maintain rapport, but in most business situations the important questions must eventually be asked if you want to avoid risk and obtain the best outcome for the company and its people, and for you. Ultimately, you'll be judged on your performance, which will be impacted significantly by the quality of your questions.

When faced with a choice of whether or not to ask a question, I think of it this way:

If the question elicits a problem or weakness in a strategy or proposal, or if it generates a better solution, then the question is useful.

If the question validates a decision or course of action, and doubt is reduced or removed, then the question is also useful.

In other words, nothing is lost by questions being asked, except perhaps a little time, and some pride for the person who might not be able to satisfactorily answer the questions; but everything can be lost by not asking the questions – not just money and share value, but also reputation, jobs, opportunities and perhaps the entire business.

The next chapter, *Clarifying Meaning - Fuzzy Language*, outlines the framework for the **Powerful Questions,** and then we'll look at the **Powerful Questions**, how they work and how to use them.

- **Never be afraid to ask the challenging questions.**

- **Always have the courage to ask challenging questions.**

- **Always be willing to answer challenging questions.**

- **Always support those who have the courage to ask challenging questions -**
  they may save your neck and the business.

1

Clarifying Meaning -
Fuzzy Language

Chapter 1

CLARIFYING MEANING - FUZZY LANGUAGE

I f you look through the positions vacant ads for managers and executives you'll see several common, high-ranking requirements for the applicant, of which 'excellent communications skills' is usually one. 'Excellent influencing skills' is close behind.

The majority of miscommunication in business arises from the use of fuzzy language.

Most employers and employees would agree that communication skills are important in business. Communication and connection between people within the organization, or with people outside the organization, is the lifeblood of the business.

The majority of miscommunication in business arises from the use of fuzzy language.

What is 'fuzzy' language?

Fuzzy language is non-specific, general, global, broadly encompassing, often abstract or vague language.

Fuzzy language usually does not clearly define the subject or process that it describes - language that:

- has more than one meaning (e.g. 'glass')

- refers to more than one thing ('people')

- describes a class ('dog')

- is equally descriptive of two or more things that are distinguishable in the detail ('boat' – a red boat, a blue boat, a motor boat, a sail boat)

- is descriptive of a series of events or actions ('implemented')

- does not have sufficient sensory data to enable the listener to match the sensory representations of the speaker ('beautiful').

An example of 'fuzzy' language is the one mentioned above - 'excellent communication skills'. Its meaning is unclear. How is an applicant supposed to know what that means in the context of the particular job that is advertised? Yet knowing which skills are necessary is an important consideration in writing a resumé and attending an interview. Referring to the wrong skills could mean that the candidate misses out on the job.

Each candidate who applies will consider that they have 'excellent communication skills'. They may have excellent communication skills, but not necesarily the specific communication skills or style required to perform in the specific role.

The recruitment firm must be able to match the candidate's communication skills to the communication skills set required by its client.

The more specific the meaning and understanding of each party as to what constitutes excellent communication for the client's

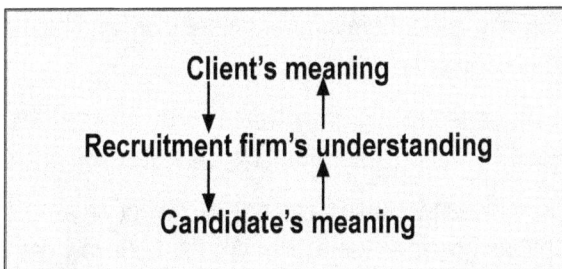

Client's meaning

↓ ↑

Recruitment firm's understanding

↓ ↑

Candidate's meaning

business purposes, the more likely that a match will be found.

As long as one party, in this case the recruitment firm, knows how to ask the right questions to clarify the meaning of the client's or candidate's fuzzy language, the desired outcome is likely to be achieved. However, if the parties do not have that questioning skill, the end result is likely to be a mismatch between the client and the candidate, with consequential loss/cost to the client and the recruitment firm, and probably also to the candidate.

Facts, perceptions and meaning

When I was at law school, I heard the story of a dramatic demonstration by a law professor who arranged for his lecture to be interrupted by actors dressed as masked bandits. The bandits created chaos for a few minutes and then left the lecture room. The students were not aware beforehand of the impending raid. After the raid, and the students had settled back down, they were asked to describe in writing what had happened, what they observed and what they heard.

No two of the 50 or so students agreed on the details of what had occurred. They may as well have been watching 50 different sets of actors.

They were all in the same room, and were able to see and hear what happened, but somehow they did not relate the same story.

The facts were common to all in the room, but they perceived the events differently, gave them different meanings, and held different beliefs and opinions about the facts.

If cameras had been rolling, they would have depicted the facts – what happened – without interpretation, bias, deletion or distortion.

The human mind and senses are not as objective as a camera. Our perceptions are very subjective. We filter our raw perceptions through our experiences, attitudes and beliefs to create our reality.

```
                    ┌─────────┐
                    │ Common  │
                    │  Facts  │
                    └─────────┘
          ↙                           ↘
┌──────────────┐              ┌──────────────┐
│     A's      │              │     B's      │
│   Meaning,   │              │   Meaning,   │
│   Opinion,   │              │   Opinion,   │
│    Belief,   │              │    Belief,   │
│  Perception  │              │  Perception  │
└──────────────┘              └──────────────┘
```

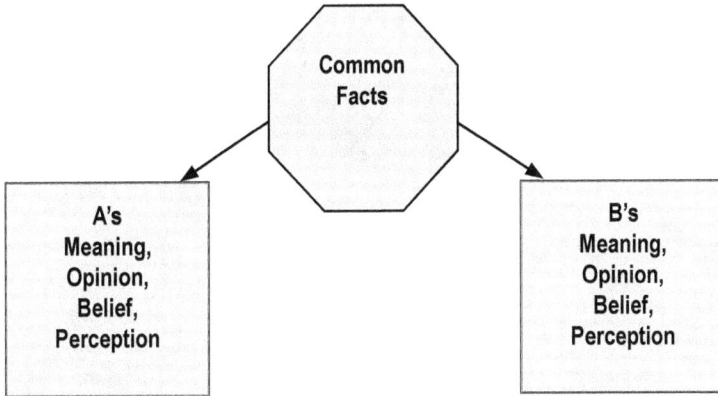

The meaning that one person ascribes to an event or conversation is often very different to the meaning ascribed by someone else who was present at the same time; and both are often different from the meaning intended by the speaker. Add to that the possibility of errors of perception on the part of the speaker, and you have a strong likelihood that what was once a simple set of facts will become a complex mass of erroneous understanding.

That phenomenon is common in business. After any meeting there will be differences of opinion as to what was said, even though the people at the meeting heard the same words and may even have taken notes or minutes. More often than not, the notes and minutes are interpretations of the events and conversations.

Even more common is the situation where two or more people do not experience exactly the same facts, but there is some overlap – they may, for instance, have been present at some meetings together, but not at all the meetings about a particular topic.

In business, it is inevitable that two or more people will share some experiences and not others. One Director may have ridden out a recession successfully, and another may have been burned. They will probably look at certain risks in very different ways. One may say "This is a manageable risk", the other may say "No, it's too risky".

31

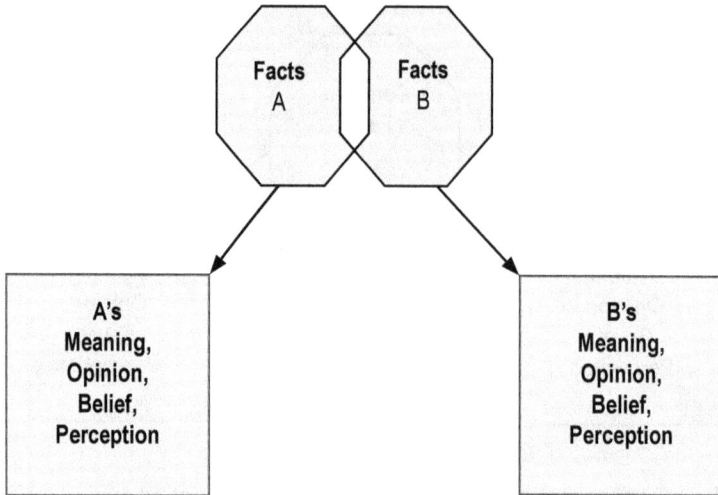

They think they are talking about the same thing, whereas in fact they are not. They are not talking about the proposal before them. They are talking about their own experience, perceptions and beliefs, and unless they can identify the facts upon which they base their views, they will probably never agree on an outcome.

The same principle applies when an executive or manager agrees to a proposal, or accepts a report, in which fuzzy language is used.

The person making the presentation has a unique set of experiences, beliefs and attitudes that colour their perspective. The person hearing the presentation has a very different set of experiences, beliefs and attitudes through which the presentation is filtered. Although the dictionary definition of the words used can be agreed, the actual meaning for each person is likely to be different.

Consider the following scenario: You are about to have a discussion with Ben, one of your young managers, following lengthy and expensive negotiations, conducted on your company's behalf by Ben.

In the past, Ben has demonstrated his ability to successfully negotiate moderately important deals. This was his chance to hit the big time.

Your impression of Ben is that he is a 'straight shooter' with you, and is not afraid to speak the truth. You believe that the other party is very interested in the deal being offered and that it would be to their advantage, as well as yours.

You: *"How did the discussions go?"*

Ben: *"Not so good. I suspected all along that they were not really interested and that seems to have been a correct assessment. We had lengthy discussions where I presented the proposal and answered their questions, but in the end they said that they weren't interested because they couldn't make money out of the idea. I think we'd be best to scrap that alliance and find someone else to do the deal with. I thought that perhaps Smith & Co might be an ideal partner. What do you think?"*

When Ben entered your office, you were fairly certain that Ben would present a successful deal to you.

Ben's description of events came as a bit of a shock to you, and has shifted your whole awareness. Ben seems confident that he has understood the discussions, and it's clear that he believes that dealing with the previous party is a pointless exercise. His brief report has withdrawn your conceptual engagement from the expected alliance with your preferred partner, created the possibility of a new alliance and re-directed your awareness to Smith and Co. Ben has asked for your thoughts on Smith & Co's involvement in the deal, and his question engages your awareness in that new possibility.

Has Ben told you the truth?

The answer is yes – from his perspective. But if you'd been a fly on the wall at the discussions, you may have formed a different view of the other party's position and intention. And if you'd been able to see inside Ben's mind you'd be aware that Ben has changed reality quite effortlessly and probably without realising how he did it, resulting in the loss of a possible opportunity and wasted investment in negotiations to date.

Lets have a sneak look into Ben's flow of consciousness:

Other party: *"At this stage we don't see a way to make money out of this proposal. We can't do the deal."*

Choices Ben made:

Perception: Did I hear that comment clearly? At that moment I was thinking about his previous comment. Will I ask for it to be repeated? No, I'm pretty sure that I caught the gist of it. It's what I suspected all along. They don't think they can make money.

Meaning: I think they said 'At this stage', so maybe there is a possibility of doing a deal in the future. On the other hand, I've heard that before, and I've said it many times when I really meant 'no'. I think that they were just being polite. What it means is that they don't want to do business. They said 'No deal'.

Processing: They've given us a hard time ever since we started this negotiation. The more I think about it, the more I realise that this whole exercise was a waste of time. They really aren't interested. We'd be better to scrap this potential partner and find another partner.

Memorising: (On the plane) I have to explain this to my boss tomorrow. Let me write it down, so that I have the facts right. What did they say? I think it was something like "We can't make money out of this idea. It's no deal."

Recall: (Next day, in your office – you ask "How did the discussions go?"). The words "We can't make money out of this idea" arise in Ben's mind along with the meaning "They aren't interested". The rest of the discussions fade into obscurity in Ben's memory as being irrelevant.

Description: (Ben – congruent and confident):"Not so good. I suspected all along that they were not really interested and that seems to have been a correct assessment. We had lengthy discussions where I presented the proposal and answered their questions, but in the end they said that they weren't interested because they couldn't make money out of the idea. I think we'd be best to scrap that alliance and find someone else to do the deal with. I thought that perhaps Smith & Co might be an ideal partner. What do you think?"

Did Ben accurately describe what the other party said? No. But he still related his version with an honest intention. Ben's version was a distortion of what was said. Ben did not report the facts, and if you accept what he says at face value you may be tempted to make a decision that writes off the time and money invested in negotiations so far, and to arrange a deal with a less effective partner. A good opportunity could be lost.

Multiple filters

Now imagine how the negotiations would be described if Ben reported to Anne, who in turn reports to you. Anne has no direct knowledge of what was said at the negotiations. She relies on Ben to inform her of the discussions and you rely on Anne to inform you.

It is likely that Anne's report to you will be distorted even further, according to Anne's perception of what Ben told her, the meaning Anne ascribes to what Ben said, how she processed, memorised and recalls that data, and the way she chooses to describe the events to you.

Ben is now out of range of questions. You don't want to be accused of micro-managing Anne's section, so you don't call Ben in to answer questions. Assumptions become facts and your decision is made on inaccurate data.

A few days later you receive a call from the executive of the company with whom Ben originally negotiated.   He expresses surprise that your company walked away from negotiations when all that he wanted was more substantiation of how the figures were calculated and how the figures would be achieved. Until that was done, they couldn't entertain the deal.

You recall a childhood story of the English wartime lieutenant who sent a message by courier relay to command headquarters: "*Send reinforcements, we're going to advance.*" By the time the final courier in the relay reached the General two days later, the message was "*Send three and fourpence, we're going to a dance.*"

When you think back to Ben's message, you realise that all the clues were there, embedded in his language, highlighting which questions you could have asked to ensure that you had the facts, or at least identifying where you needed to gather more facts.

In that situation should Ben's boss blame Ben for the stuff up? He could, but this is potentially a learning exercise for both of them. Ben needs to learn how to listen clearly, be aware of the way he processes data, and learn when and how to ask questions that clarify what is said; his boss might decide to take a leaf out of Graeme Kraehe's book and not necessarily accept the information that is presented to him, to learn how to ensure that his mind isn't hijacked away from the underlying issues, and learn how to ask questions that get to the facts.

How often does this scenario happen in business? Every day, in every company. Leaders must have the confidence, and competence, to stay present with the real issues, and to ask questions that probe, elicit, clarify and verify the facts, assumptions, processes and meaning contained in written documents and in conversations.

Accurate Communication

Accurate communication requires that the speaker and listener, or writer and reader, each has the same internal representation and meaning of the words used. Accuracy and common meaning are rarely achieved when unclear, ambiguous, fuzzy language is involved. When you hear or read the words such as:

> *We are short listed for a number of projects that should commence shortly,*

or

> *Negotiations have begun on the outstanding amount.*

or

> *Couple this with changing business priorities and other major project initiatives, and the current business case no longer represents a realisable and clear benefit stream and does not accord with the group's emerging strategic priorities,*

you are almost certainly not sharing the same meaning as the speaker. If more detail is not given by the speaker to explain what they mean or are doing, you must be prepared to ask questions to elicit that information.

Who is responsible for clarifying meaning - the speaker or the listener?

If you are the speaker

If you are *presenting* the information to someone else, the meaning of your communication is their meaning, what they understand you to mean. Your responsibility is to make your meaning clear to them, if you want agreement or correct action.

If they walk away with a different understanding of your proposal to what you intended, are they responsible for the error? No. Your job is to ensure that they are listening, and that you transfer your meaning to their mind. Only when that is achieved have you communicated clearly. If you don't communicate your meaning clearly, you are unlikley to obtain the outcome that you want.

There are a number of ways to do that, including matching their preferred senses and learning style, or asking them for feedback as to what they understand by what you presented, or how the proposal fits their needs. Inevitably, you'll need to ask questions that identify the other person's internal reality.

The basic rule is this:

> **The meaning of your communication
> is the response that you get**

If someone thinks you are talking about chickens but you are actually talking about turkeys, the meaning (to them) of your communication is....chickens.

It's your responsibility to get feedback and adjust your communication until your message is clearly understood by the other party.

If you are the listener

If you are the *listener*, then you are the person to whom the message is being delivered and it is your understanding that is at stake and from which you will make decisions. It is a subjective criterion, not an objective one. Your understanding will be based on your experiences and map of reality, your frames of reference, and your expectations, which may be very different from the picture that the speaker has in his or her head.

If the information being presented to you is important for you to be able to make a decision or take action, then it is your responsibility to ensure that you understand facts and issues sufficiently to make the right decision or to take the right action.

Don't expect the speaker to read your mind – from their perspective, what they are saying makes sense. Ask the questions that will make sense (to you) of the conversation or document.

That will entail your asking questions to elicit the meaning intended by the speaker.

> **If you are the listener or reader, the meaning of the communication is the other person's (speaker's or writer's) meaning.**

If you want to understand the meaning, it is your responsibility (to yourself) to obtain clarification.

That statement may seem strange at first, because we are used to hearing that the speaker must be clear. However, if you are in a leadership or decision-making role and you are going to rely on what is said or written, you must be prepared to probe, challenge and clarify what is said.

That usually means asking questions.

You are in command of communication

As both speaker and as listener, you are in control of the quality of the communication.

So, what this means is that, as both speaker and as listener, you are in control of the quality of the communication. You can clarify for the other person what you mean, and you can obtain clarification from the other person of what they mean. You need never again misunderstand others, or be misunderstood! In business, that means you and the people with whom you interact will be more effective and it will result in significant savings of time and money, and much less frustration and angst.

Fuzzometer

We each have an inbuilt 'fuzzometer' that can detect fuzzy language. Some call it a BS detector. Others simply call it a gut feel that tells them something isn't quite right. Many call it intuition.

Whatever it is called, the fuzzometer works on the principle of movements or gaps in awareness. You can enhance and fine tune your fuzzometer by learning to observe what happens to your awareness, your consciousness, when, for example:

- you hear fuzzy language as compared to specific language

- something is left unsaid and leaves a gap in information

- something that is said just doesn't add up

- what is said diverts your attention from the crucial issues

- you are on the receiving end of 'spin'

- someone is not taking responsibility.

The ability to observe your own mind operate is one of the greatest skills a leader can have. It is at the core of the dictum Know Thyself.

In mystical traditions, the dictum would read 'Know Thy Self', because at the moment of observing your awareness, you are the witness of the flow of consciousness – the 'I' or Self observing itself at play.

John Grinder, co-founder of NLP (Neurolinguistic Programming) once told me that true genius is the ability to observe your own mind. He's right. From that witness state **The ability to observe your own mind operate is one of the greatest skills a leader can have.** it is possible to expand, contract, direct and focus awareness effortlessly. It is the source of mastery of mind, from which the Zen 'effortless effort' of the peak state of performance arises. In sports it is known as 'the zone'.

It is also a common experience in business that often arises from the speed, rhythm and intensity of the deal, and from the challenge of creating something new or different, something that requires that we expand our awareness beyond the known reality to create a new product, a new service, a new process or exploit a new market. It is, essentially, a state of awareness that transcends our usual awareness.

Einstein, Edison and Tesla are three of the genius minds of the past. Edison had only several years of schooling. Einstein flunked school. Tesla was the only one of the three to have a strong formal education. Yet all three transformed our world in a very practical sense, each was very successful in his field and vast industries have grown around their work (including General Electric, one of the largest corporations in the world).

Read their writings and biographies and one thing stands out – they all had the knack of expanding their awareness to conceive an idea that was impossible at the time, and then to contract, direct and focus their awareness and energy to focus on the specifics required for a functional outcome, such as the light globe (Edison), alternating current (Tesla) and $E=MC^2$ (Einstein).

Unfortunately, many companies have cultures that stifle their people's ability to tap into the genius state. Fortunately, the genius state, the ability to observe our own minds, is personal and can be developed in any circumstances by anyone.

For the purposes of the techniques in this book, all that is required is to recognise when language expands, contracts, directs and focuses your awareness.

The *speaker's* language will follow and reflect their processes of awareness. If their awareness expands, their language will be fuzzier. If their awareness contracts, their language will be more specific. If their awareness is specifically directed and focussed, their language will be more sensory specific. If their awareness shifts direction or focus, so will their language.

The *listener's* awareness will follow the language of the speaker. Global (fuzzy) language will cause the listener's awareness to expand. Specific language will cause the listener's awareness to contract. A shift in direction or focus of the language will cause the listener's awareness to re-direct or focus.

This is the subtle art behind the skill of influencing and persuading others.

The power of fuzzy language

The beauty, power and effectiveness of fuzzy language lies in its ability to

➢ embrace multiple meanings in a word or phrase,

➢ economically describe a range of related or similar things, behaviours or outcomes,

➢ expand awareness and inspire.

However, as with all forms of power, it can be used for positive benefits, or it can be abused - used to the detriment of others. Fuzzy language is one of the favourite tools of leaders, motivators, public relations and advertising consultants, sales people, politicians, con artists and anyone adept at persuasion and influence.

It is important to realise that there are many reasons why people use fuzzy language. Some use it with integrity, and others don't.

Some reasons why people use fuzzy language

Not able to be specific	Are guessing
To motivate and empower	Aren't sure if they are right
Communicate to masses	To obscure real intention & facts
Don't have enough information	Don't want to be specific
To save time	To avoid responsibility

Fuzzy language can be useful

Fuzzy language is a shorthand way of describing something that may be quite complex. It is a necessary part of efficient communication, by which we can save time by using the fuzzy words in contexts where they are well understood by the listener or reader.

There are times when a leader will need to use fuzzy language, such as to convey a message of possibility and inspiration to many people. The fact that the words can mean a number of things to different people allows us to ascribe to those words whatever meaning makes sense to us, and makes it easier to reach agreement.

We often choose to relate what we are thinking in global terms, not specifics. This can be because of the exigencies of time and other pressures, or perhaps because we think that the other person understands the facts and/or meaning of our words.

A complex meeting with convoluted interactions may be abbreviated to a shorthand version:

We discussed the issues

or

We negotiated in accordance with our planned approach but the other side would not budge.

Both those examples tell you very little about what happened. They may be sufficient description in a particular context, but they are not very useful if you want to know why the negotiations failed. If the fuzzy, global language does not make sense to the degree necessary for you to be able to properly understand what is being said, or to take clear action, you must know how to ask questions that elicit the necessary details.

Continuum

Specific and fuzzy language patterns are at either end of a continuum/spectrum.

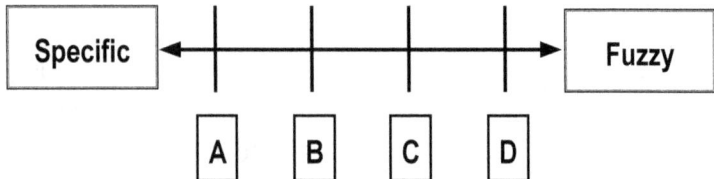

There can be varying degrees of specific/fuzzy language between the two extremes. Language at point A can be very precise, clear and unambiguous but can also be so specific and defining of its subject matter as to be pedantic, losing sight of context, missing the whole perspective and the relationship with the big picture.

Language at point C on the continuum is more global than specific, significantly fuzzier than language at point B, but clearer than language at point D.

Language at point D can be uplifting, elevating and inspiring, almost poetic, but can also be so abstract as to be almost meaningless. Definition of subject matter can be virtually non-existent, leaving the listener's mind to roam free and ascribe whatever meaning it wants to the language.

In any situation where you want to achieve an outcome from your communication, it is useful to

- understand the difference between specific and global language,

- (if you are the listener) be aware of when one or the other is being used by others

- (if you are the speaker) be aware of when it is most useful for you to use more specific or more general language.

It is *particularly* useful to be aware of when a shift occurs from fuzzy to specific or vice-versa.

'Specific' = sensory data

Fuzzy language contains less sensory information than specific language. When language is specific, it contains more sensory data that we can convert into internal sensory representations of the language.

When language is specific, it contains more sensory data.

The senses take in data. We relate to the world via our senses. We perceive (see, hear, feel, smell and taste) the world around us with varying degrees of accuracy and then convert that information into internal representations in our consciousness, with varying degrees of precision.

The internal representations are not factual, but are meanings shaped by our beliefs, attitudes and map of reality. That includes our values and culture - what is rude in one culture may be acceptable in another. Something was said or done – that is the fact. The meaning ascribed to that fact depends on what filters are applied. Some filters are personal, some cultural.

When we relate (communicate) our experience to others we are actually relating our internal representation of the original sensory data, this time with varying degrees of quality of recollection. Memory can be notoriously unreliable if the event being recalled was not of significance at the time it was perceived.

Memory is especially unreliable if there is a large amount of data to process and recall. What the mind does in that case is to gather the bits of information into categories of items and recall the categories rather than the bits (chunks) of information. In other words, the mind generalises and summarises the data, such as saying "Africa" instead of naming every (specific) country in Africa.

The process of clarification via sensory description

The sentence in the following box is high on the 'fuzzometer'.

> **We attended the meeting, but couldn't reach
> a satisfactory arrangement.**

Notice, in the diagram on the right, how each component can be made clearer by adding sensory specific language to the description of the meeting.

As we shall see, fuzzy language can be fairly meaningless, particularly if you want to know why something didn't work and to find a solution. For that, you must delve into the specifics. In the example above, the key senses by which the negotiations were perceived are probably the visual and auditory senses – what was seen and heard.

In that example, a higher degree of specificity can be achieved by describing the behaviours and words of those present at the negotiations. When you elicit the data about what was said and done in the negotiations, you'll be better able to understand the reason why the negotiation did not work, and how to improve it.

So when we ask for specifics, we are actually asking for sensory data that 'makes sense' through one or more of our senses - the facts without deletion, distortion or embellishment, so far as humanly possible.

Clarity = Specifics = Sensory Data = Facts.

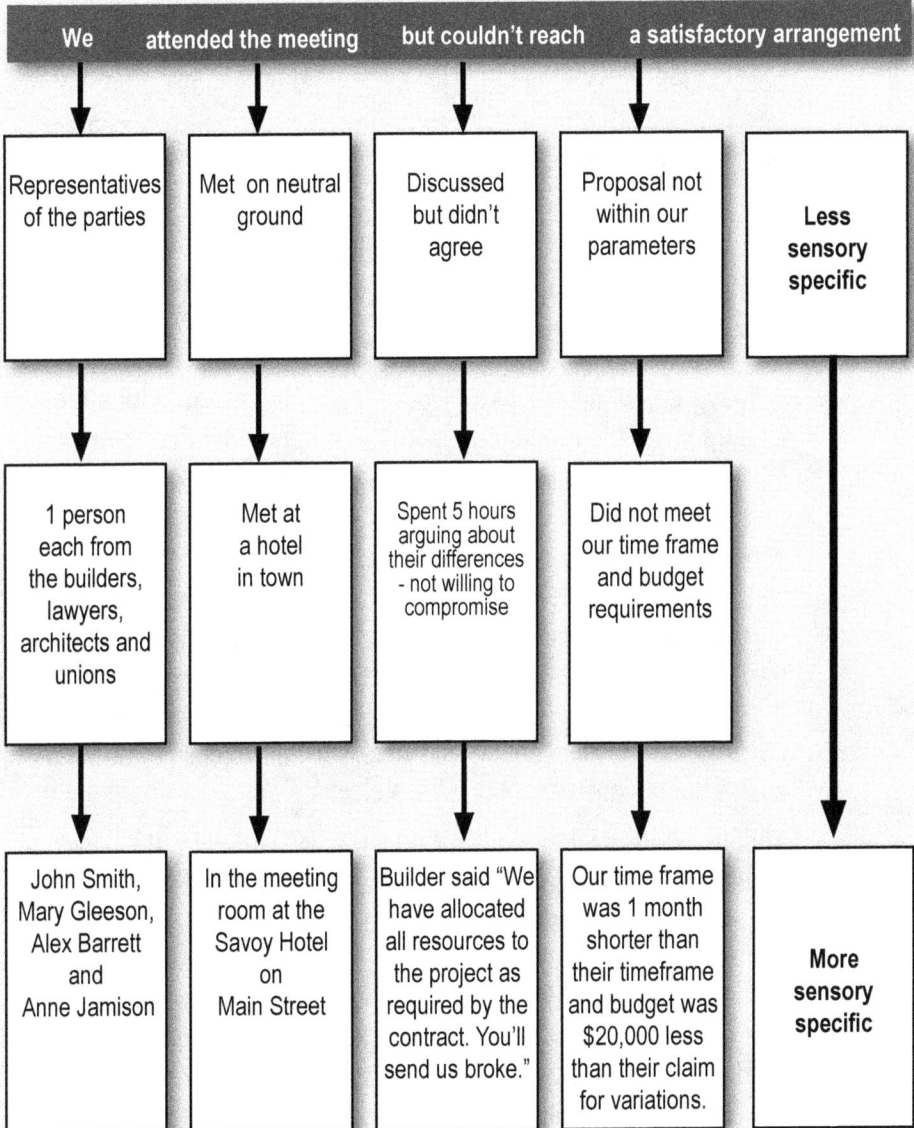

We	attended the meeting	but couldn't reach	a satisfactory arrangement	
Representatives of the parties	Met on neutral ground	Discussed but didn't agree	Proposal not within our parameters	**Less sensory specific**
1 person each from the builders, lawyers, architects and unions	Met at a hotel in town	Spent 5 hours arguing about their differences - not willing to compromise	Did not meet our time frame and budget requirements	
John Smith, Mary Gleeson, Alex Barrett and Anne Jamison	In the meeting room at the Savoy Hotel on Main Street	Builder said "We have allocated all resources to the project as required by the contract. You'll send us broke."	Our time frame was 1 month shorter than their timeframe and budget was $20,000 less than their claim for variations.	**More sensory specific**

Quantum Effect in business communication

In quantum physics there exists a curious phenomenon: the quanta – the bundles of energy that make up physical matter – exist in potential in all possible locations until the scientist observes them, at which point they take a definite location and form the scientist's view of reality. Human consciousness, when focused on the possibilities, causes one of the infinite, concurrent possibilities to be selected. The other possibilities still exist, but one is selected and locked into our awareness, which becomes our reality (or 'real').

Fuzzy language is similar – it has numerous potential, subtly different meanings until such time as the listener focuses on a specific meaning, at which point the fuzzy language begins to make sense in that limited form, i.e. is seen, heard, felt, smelled and tasted in accordance with the world-map of the listener. It takes shape in our consciousness as a recognisable form to which we relate, and becomes tangible. Go to court any day and you will hear this effect manifested during a trial. The witnesses will give opposing views of the same circumstances, each swearing that they are telling the truth. You'll see the same situation in harrassment, discrimination and unfair dismissal claims, as well as in worker's compensation stress claims.

Fuzzy language is similar – it has numerous potential, subtly different meanings until such time as the listener focuses on a specific meaning.

This is where asking the right question is important. If we ask questions that assume that a certain perspective is true we'll simply attract the answers that we expected. That phenomenon is common in investigations, where an initial theory or perception is formed that colours the objectivity of the investigator. The evidence that fits the theory is then more visible, because the mind scans for data that is consistent with the perceived reality. This is part of the Reticular Activating System, a function of our awareness that seeks out that which is consistent with our current understanding and our current perceived reality.

The evidence then supports the theory or perception, which becomes more concrete as the evidence adds up to prove the case.

If, on the other hand, we challenge the accepted wisdom or an assumption to see if it is true, we might find a whole new approach that is truly innovative and groundbreaking. That was what happened in 1982 when two Australian scientists, Barry J. Marshall and Robin Warren asserted that duodenal and gastric ulcers were caused by bacteria. The established wisdom handed down from generation to generation of medical practitioners worldwide prior to 1982 had been that ulcers were caused by stress. That idea was so entrenched that nobody could believe that ulcers were caused by bacteria and it took some years for Marshall and Warren to gain support for the idea, even though the proof was in the lab results. In 2005 they were awarded the Nobel Prize for their discovery.

Questions provide an excellent means for directing awareness to a specific choice out of all the possible realities that are available in business, and for breaking us out of limited mindsets, beliefs and assumptions that prevent us from creating the as yet unknown.

Why is it useful to be able to detect the shift from specific to fuzzy language?

A single word or a single phrase may be fuzzy. A sentence or an entire paragraph can also be fuzzy.

Usually you'll find that within a sentence or a paragraph, some of the words and phrases are fuzzy and others are more specific. In business, the more the 'fuzzometer' registers 'high', the more cautious you need to be.

One of the most important skills that highly effective business leaders have is to be able (as listener or reader) to detect when language shifts along the specific/fuzzy continuum.

One of the most important skills that highly effective business leaders have is to be able to detect when language shifts along the specific/ fuzzy continuum.

When I practised law, particularly when conducting trials, which required the evidence to be scrutinised and facts elicited, I noticed that a witness might at times relate events with considerable detail, and at other times would give broad general descriptions or give summaries of the events that he or she witnessed.

Quite often the fuzzier, broad descriptions were mixed in with the specific detail, which made the fuzzy parts seem more plausible, or easier to overlook. Specific details usually suggested that the witness had paid attention and recollected more accurately than one who could only provide a general impression.

It wasn't long before I began to realise that the point at which a witness shifted from more specific to more fuzzy was a strong indicator that I ought to ask questions of that part of the testimony.

Sometimes the questions led to innocuous answers, or to sufficient facts to verify the witness's testimony, but in the vast majority of cases the questions revealed that the witness either did not know the facts relating to the 'fuzzy' section of their evidence, was unclear as to what they had seen or heard, or preferred to avoid that part of the evidence. The shift to fuzzy language was a cover for the gaps in the witness's testimony.

A simple example of how language can shift along the continuum might be when describing a holiday:

"We flew on British Airways to New York, where we stayed sightseeing for a week before hiring a car and driving up

to Niagara Falls. We stayed there for 2 days with some friends, then hired a car and drove all the way to California.

We took an excursion to Mexico for a couple of days, then back to L.A. We then went to Asia for a while and after that to Italy where we took our time driving to the various cities of interest such as Rome, Venice, Florence and Milan, taking in the culture, history and traditions of each place..."

Did you notice where there was a substantial shift in the level of specificity? If not, have a look at it again and notice how easily the shift can be buried in the rest of the description.The section "We took an excursion to Mexico for a couple of days" is less specific than the previous two sentences, but the next section is even fuzzier (less specific) "We then went to Asia for a while", which does not provide details of location or time frame.

Notice that some of the words and phrases used are fuzzier than others: "we stayed", "sightseeing", "driving up to", "drove all the way", "an excursion", "a couple of days" are all capable of further clarification. Each could mean a number of different things or could be performed a number of different ways.

A less specific, more global, fuzzier version of the same holiday might be:

"We flew to the USA. From there we went to Japan, India Turkey and Italy, Germany, France and the UK."

Here, the USA and Japanese legs are dealt with briefly in contrast to the first version. This shorter treatment of the journey is no less correct, simply less specific.

Whereas with the first version, it is possible to form a picture in your mind's eye that corresponds in more detail to what is in the mind of the relator of the journey, in this second version the description only enables your mind to picture a map of the USA, then a broad map of Japan and so forth – in other words, you are visualising the whole countries as if from a satellite or as if on a globe or map, with little detail and less engagement to the story. You have no idea where the person travelled, or even how they travelled.

In order to take in the whole country, you must take a global or expanded perspective, just as a CEO or Board must be able to take an expanded perspective of their company, strategy, market and even the corporate timeline over the next 20 years instead of only the next month.

The next level of fuzziness may be something like:

"We holidayed in the USA, Asia and Europe."

The fuzziest version might be:

"We travelled around the world."

People who are skilled at avoiding responsibility are skilled at making that type of shift without it being noticed.

The same principle applies when the shift is from global to specific as it does with shifts from specific to global – a shift in either direction provides a good starting point for questions. When someone uses language that goes global ⟶ specific, they will often appear to the listener to be cooperative, knowledgeable and trustworthy. However, the shift from global to specific can also mean that someone is directing and focusing our awareness on a particular aspect of discussion with the effect of diverting attention from another aspect that may deserve questions. When details are provided, the reality being described becomes more concrete, and the mind becomes more contracted and focused around the reality being described and more engaged with that reality. We are then less likely to question other aspects of the issue.

Business application

When I changed career to corporate consulting in the 1980's, I found the same thing happening in the business environment.

I still asked a lot of questions, though for a different purpose and not in an interrogating manner. Again, the shift in language between specific ⟵⟶ fuzzy was a clear indicator that questions needed to be asked.

In a business and personal context, the shift between specific and fuzzy can mean various things, including that the other person involved in the conversation is

- not taking responsibility

- avoiding an issue

- pretending to have the facts or an answer when in fact they did not

- being manipulative

- deleting important information

- attempting to create an impression that serves their agenda ('spin').

It can also indicate deliberate lies. More often than not, however, the other person is simply not clear about what they are saying – they do not have sufficient data or have not thought things through thoroughly, or perhaps they have given the matter a lot of thought but have not come up with a suitable solution. Whatever the reason, they resort to generalisations, or focus on the details of one element of the matter under discussion to distract the listener from the part they wish to avoid. A simple matter of trying to save face.

More often than not, however, the other person is simply not clear about what they are saying.

Either way, it doesn't help the business.

How people use the specific/fuzzy continuum to cover up these motives will become clearer as you read the examples in this book.

Board and Executive levels

Similar communication issues are found at Board and executive levels. If anything, the language at Board and executive levels is more global and strategic, and less specific, than at operational levels because the topics under discussion at Board and executive levels are the '*big picture*' items, which by their nature are defined by '*big picture*', global language that connects or embraces many interconnecting elements under one umbrella by expanding the listener's awareness.

The stakes are also higher, of course, and it is essential that Directors and executives know how to ask the questions that count - the questions that probe, challenge, verify and clarify the necessary detail and meaning to enable them to make informed decisions. If they don't, a great deal of money can be lost when a strategy doesn't work, a proposal is based on unworkable assumptions, or a report on which they rely is defective.

The Power underlying *Powerful Questions*

Before we go into the various techniques of the *Powerful Questions*, I'll explain some of the principles that drive the power in the *Powerful Questions*. These principles are rarely mentioned in business courses, possibly because they are not easily reduced to intellectual modelling, but are best understood through our inner experience.

There is a quiet evolution occurring in business worldwide that recognises that there is something more to business, performance and being human than the models that we've been accustomed to in the past. Companies are realising that we need different models and skills to deal with the way that business is changing. They recognise that there is 'something else' that is necessary to be successful in business over the next twenty years. The following is part of that 'something else'.

Language and awareness

In July 2003 Business Week Magazine published an article about work life and the workplace entitled *Zen and the Art of Corporate Productivity* in which the authors outlined how corporations are offering meditation courses to their employees. The article noted that corporate interest in meditation arose from the findings of The National Institutes of Health, the University of Massachusetts and Harvard University that meditation enhances certain qualities that companies need from their knowledge workers – increased creativity, enhanced intuition, optimised concentration for multi-tasking, and reduced stress.

The classic definition of meditation is to 'still the fluctuations and chatter of the mind'.

'Stilling' the mind is a practice found in most spiritual and martial arts traditions. When this practice is mastered, the adept can slow down the processes that generate thought and observe how a thought arises, reshapes, evolves, and dissolves.

Those who have been able to master that practice describe the process by which a seed of an idea arises from an unformed source, called consciousness, and then begins to form into a clear, recognizable thought. We become aware of the seed idea, and observe it develop within our mind. As the thought develops and takes shape it gains solidity, 'realness'. We then label it, first in thought, and then in internal dialogue, and finally in written or spoken words. When we label something, it takes on an independent reality, which is precisely why we need tools such as the **Powerful Questions** to ensure that we are dealing with the same reality when communicating with each other.

Hellen Keller, the blind and deaf girl who achieved so much in her life, wrote about the concrete reality that follows labelling. Before she lost her sight and hearing at 18 months of age through an illness, she had learned the word 'water', but not many other words. At the age of seven, her teacher, Anne Sullivan, began teaching her words, by marking out the letters for words with her fingers in Helen's palm and attempting to associate the words with objects. Helen learned to move her own fingers in the shape of the letters, but had no idea that she was spelling a word or even that words existed. One day, Anne Sullivan took Helen out of the house. Helen eventually learned to touch type, and later described the circumstances in her autobiography, *The Story of My Life*:

> *[Anne Sullivan] brought me my hat and I knew I was going out into the warm sunshine. This thought, if a wordless sensation may be called a thought, made me hop and skip with pleasure....We walked down a path to the well... Someone was drawing water and my teacher placed my hand under the spout...and spelled into the other hand the word 'water'....Suddenly I felt a misty consciousness as of something forgotten...and somehow the mystery of language was revealed to me. I knew then what w-a-t-e-r meant...That living word awakened my soul...Everything had a name, and each name gave birth to a new thought. As we returned to the house, every object which I touched seemed to quiver with life. That was because I saw everything with the strange, new sight that had come to me.*

The progression from seed in consciousness to solid reality and vocalised words happens in nanoseconds, and goes unnoticed by most of us, drowned by the background static of 'busy-ness'.

We experience a similar process when reading a book or listen to a conversation (or having words written on our palm). We read or hear the words, the words trigger a seed of an idea in our awareness, we match them to our internal representation of their meaning based on our life experience, beliefs and map of reality, then form thoughts around that meaning, and language to describe the thoughts (e.g. "That's right", or "I don't agree"). We may also at some time externalise the language in writing or verbally to convey to others our understanding of what we read or heard.

In this way the flow of consciousness is transmitted via verbal or written communication to others. One original thought can be replicated many times in that manner. Each time that the thought is transferred to, and accepted by, another person (communicated), it becomes part of a greater, more widespread reality until eventually, when critical mass is achieved, the thought becomes part of the beliefs and culture of a significant community, including business communities, or companies.

Awareness shapes language. Language shapes awareness

Questions

Questions are a highly effective means of communicating and are a fundamental tool for any business leader. They are especially powerful as a means for influencing and shaping awareness.

Questions can be used to

- gather information
- challenge and clarify thoughts
- shift perceptions, attitudes and beliefs
- build commitment, ownership and engagement of people in their organization, and
- generate change, improvement, solutions, opportunities and innovation.

Asking questions often has a far greater impact on staff engagement, ownership and commitment than if you make a statement.

For instance, what has more impact on your level of engagement – being told a fact or being asked a question that enables you to come up with the answer yourself?

What is likely to meet most resistance – being told how you have to implement change, or being asked questions that enable you to figure out how to implement change?

Did you notice, when you read the last two questions, that you changed state from a passive recipient of information to an active participant in the answer?

Questions are effective because they engage the mind, and the mind then immediately follows the process indicated by the question. Questions cause our mind to search for an answer, externally or internally.

When framed well, questions take the mind deeper, further and faster to an answer.

If you were able to observe your mind with the previous questions, you would have noticed that your awareness moved from an external focus on the page to an internal focus, scanning and directing itself towards finding the answer to the question within your inner reality. If it found the answer, it then focused on the answer and held it steady until you no longer needed it, at which point it withdrew from the answer and moved on to something else; if it didn't find an answer, you will have drawn a blank mind – no thought – a momentary 'still mind'.

The processes of directing, focusing, looking inward, looking outward, holding and withdrawing are some of the processes of consciousness that enable us to relate to our world and to ourselves, to communicate, influence and persuade, and to perform.

Processes of consciousness

Words themselves have no inherent meaning. The word 'abupati' will probably have no meaning to you, as you have no internal representation for it. If I tell you it means 'horse', then suddenly it makes sense. The meaning that we attribute to words enables words to trigger meaning in our mind. That power to trigger meaning is one of the powers of language. The meaning is the content that we hold in mind when we hear words.

However, the subtler power in language is not the meaning of the words, but the processes that the words invoke to move and shape the mind, its meanings and states of awareness. Unless you can generate that movement in others, you will not be able to influence another person's thinking. When someone else generates that movement in your mind, they influence your thinking. Poets and great orators are especially adept at using language to shift consciousness.

There are a number of ways that language influences the movement of consciousness. The following are the most applicable processes for the purposes of this book.

Key processes of consciousness		Processes for creating
Expand	Contract	Emanate
Direct (general)	Direct (specific)	
Soft Focus	Sharp Focus	Hold
Engage	Disengage	Withdraw
Internal	External	
Stillness		

Although I have split the processes into two boxes, they are intimately inter-connected processes that can 'morph' into any combination to create our reality. Basically, they are simply functions of one consciousness.

The words used in a document or conversation will generate one or more of those processes in the listener's awareness. Consider the following example from a CEO who can see an opportunity:

"When I look at this proposal I see the potential to do far better than we'd planned for the next 5 years. More profits, stronger growth, bigger market share. It gives us the capability to enter the overseas markets and build revenue in regions where the product has most demand and most value. I can see us establishing plants and staff in those countries over the next 3 or 4 years in alliance with business partners whom we've already identified and who know their local markets. We won't have to rely on our home market and in fact that will become a relatively

small part of our global market in five to ten years' time.
Each of you in this room can imagine yourself being directly
responsible for a specific region and benefiting from the
wealth that this proposal could generate."

This type of language can be very seductive. Considered as a whole, the language

- withdraws focus from the current five year plan

- substitutes (emanates) a new strategy

- directs awareness of the listeners to that new strategy

- focuses on particular aspects of the future vision while maintaining language that expands awareness

- holds the new strategy with enough general descriptions of outcomes and implementation process to give it some substance.

The speaker is unlikely to provide much detail of what the outcome would look like or how it will be achieved, because that is where there is more likely to be disagreement from the audience – for instance, in relation to the terms and conditions for taking charge of each region, or who would be responsible for a particular region.

Those issues will remain cloaked in general ('fuzzy') language that maintains an expanded awareness, encompassing many possibilities. As a result, the audience will be more likely to accept the vision held by the speaker.

If we break the paragraph down into components we can see how the language shapes the consciousness of the listener, step-by-step.

Text	Process of consciousness
When I look at this proposal I see the potential	'Potential' emanates thoughts of possibilities in the future. It expands awareness.
to do far better	'...far better...' expands awareness
than we'd planned for the next 5 years	Expands time frame, begins to withdraw awareness from existing plans and directs the listener towards a new idea
More profits, stronger growth, bigger market share.	Directs and focuses awareness on general concepts that embed and hold the idea, make it more real, but still expands: 'more', 'bigger', 'stronger'.
It gives us the capability	Emanates bigger picture, expands awareness
to enter the overseas markets and build revenue in regions where the product has most demand and most value	Directs and focuses awareness on general concepts that emanate and hold the idea, makes it more real, still using language that expands awareness.
I can see us establishing plants and staff in those countries over the next 3 or 4 years in alliance with business partners whom we've already identified and who know their local markets	Directs and focuses on general descriptions of implementation that embed and hold the idea, make it more tangible, 'real'

Text	Process of consciousness
We won't have to rely on our home market	Begins withdrawing awareness from current home market: "Won't have to rely on".
and in fact that will become a relatively small part of our global market in five to ten years' time.	Partially withdraws awareness from present circumstances. Contracts awareness relating to the current market: "In fact...will become...a small part..."
Each of you in this room	Focuses on the people in the room. Begins engaging awareness of each individual with the proposal.
can imagine	Directs consciousness to go 'internal' to emanate the images that follow, directs awareness to process internally
yourself being directly responsible for a specific region and benefiting from the wealth that this proposal could generate.	Listener becomes engaged with (immersed in) the images.

The language in this example is the language of the visionary leader and the entrepreneur – global language that expands awareness, withdraws the mind from the existing situation and transports (directs and focuses) it to another time and place.

However, sooner or later the vision must be translated into tangible, practical structures, processes and actions that create the desired reality and build the holding patterns (values, strategy, processes, systems, structure) by which the business outcome is maintained. That requires shifts of consciousness which contract, direct and focus awareness and behaviour.

The **Powerful Questions** are your tools for making those shifts.

Questions activate the core processes of consciousness

When you are aware of the shifts in your own awareness generated by language that you hear, you will immediately and intuitively know which process of consciousness has been activated, and which question to ask. That will become clearer as you read through this book.

Leaders shape consciousness

As you become more familiar with the processes of consciousness, you'll also start to use language to activate those processes in your own communications. One CEO stated:

> *"I originally learned the questions so that I could clarify what other people meant in meetings and discussions. Within a few weeks I found that there was an added benefit – when I am preparing my reports to the Board I am now very, very aware of when the language that I use is not clear, and I change it accordingly. The result is that I have fewer problems with the Board, and they have more trust for what I am saying."*

When I was writing this section, I scanned a number of books on leadership that I've collected over the years, searching for any reference to language and consciousness. There were many references to leadership communication skills, but none to the relationship between language and consciousness. The books listed many qualities and skills of leaders, but what struck me was that well over half of the skills listed related to communication and influencing, which could be described in a phrase as 'shaping human consciousness'.

**The skills of a leader include the skill
of shaping human consciousness**

In other words, we are not simply dealing with words, things, behaviours and outcomes when we communicate, but with shaping inner consciousness into patterns that enable us to think and do the things that are necessary to achieve the outcomes that we want. That model also applies to our own inner conversations with ourselves. Every other model for human performance falls within that model, whether in business, sport or any other area of life.

There are many uses for this skill in business, such as:

- implementing change in organizations

- coaching for performance

- developing a strategy

- inspiring with Vision

- instilling values

- negotiating

- resolving disagreement and conflict

- innovating

- finding solutions and opportunities.

Each of those applications requires the substitution of one thought or mindset for another – a change in content. However, to change the content of the mind we must activate different processes to create a shift of thinking, a different perspective of what might be possible.

To change the content of the mind we must activate different processes to create a shift of thinking.

In order to enable others to grasp and own a different way of thinking the leader must be able to use language, and particularly questions, to create those shifts. This skill is often called 'persuasion' or 'influencing'.

The example (given above) of the CEO's vision for a new strategy that enables the company to expand into overseas markets is an example of shaping consciousness towards the future by using fuzzy language. However, fuzzy language patterns can also be used to avoid responsibility, and the **Powerful Questions** can be used to create accountability.

Consider the following incident, which relates to a customer service issue. It happened a couple of years ago when I travelled interstate to present a workshop. See if you can identify any of the processes of consciousness, mentioned above, in the hotel reception manager's language.

A couple of months prior to the workshop I booked the five star hotel's conference facility for the workshop, and a room for myself. I was aware that the hotel may not keep the room for me if I was not checked in by 6 p.m., so I informed the hotel that I was flying into town late, and would arrive at the hotel between 9.30 p.m. and 10 p.m. Upon arrival I went to the reception desk to check in. The reception manager said:

> *"I'm very sorry, but it appears that the hotel is full, and that we don't have a room for you tonight. However I've taken the liberty of booking you into the Hyatt hotel just across the road, instead. I'll arrange for a porter to take your luggage across for you."*

The overall structure of what the manager said was quite clever. Those two sentences reflect several of the patterns described earlier. They:

- avoid giving details that may be open to criticism
- give the appearance of encompassing all aspects or issues under discussion, so that the shortcomings of an action, strategy, solution or process may not be noticed
- distort data so that the data appears to have more validity than it in fact has
- omit details so that only part of the facts are conveyed

- are very specific on a certain aspect of the situation [transfer procedure to Hyatt] so that other aspects are not questioned (both because the specifics sound like things are under control and because the specifics distract the listener from the real issues)

- appear to address an issue and then subtly shift the topic or emphasis away from the issue

- create an impression that has no factual basis.

On first reading, those patterns may not be obvious, but as you read through the book and practise the exercises, you'll find that the patterns are very easy to spot once you understand how they are constructed and delivered.

There's also another quite important element of what the manager said. Notice that

- the first sentence was designed to withdraw my mind from my expectation that I'd be staying at the hotel, and

- the second sentence was designed to emanate or create an alternative solution, and to direct and focus my awareness on staying at the Hyatt with no effort needed on my part, other than walking across the road.

In other words, the manager's statement was designed to first shift my awareness and then my actions. If he succeeds in doing that, then I'd be at the Hyatt shortly.

I had no doubt that the reception manager was presenting his case in a manner designed to persuade me to take the easy path to the Hyatt. He might have succeeded if not for the first seven words that he spoke, which set off my internal alarm bells, what I refer to as my 'fuzzometer'. Throughout the book you'll learn different ways to fine-tune your own fuzzometer by recognising shifts in other people's language and the corresponding shifts in your own awareness.

The words "*...but it appears that...*" were the main triggers for my fuzzometer. We call that pattern 'fudging'. It has no commitment, is not definitive, and involves a withdrawal from the hotel manager's personal responsibility. It is a very different statement to *"I'm very sorry. The hotel is full and there are no rooms available tonight".*

One way to challenge or clarify fudging is to ask:

*It **appears** that the hotel is full - or it **is** full?*

The word 'that' in this context also indicates I'm about to receive an interpretation of, or 'spin' on, the circumstances rather than facts. You'll see this in later chapters when we discuss how to clarify conversations, e.g. if someone says *"They said that..."*, then you will almost certainly hear an interpretation of a conversation, not the actual words used (the fact) in the conversation.

The reception manager compounded that phrase with *"...and that we don't have a room for you tonight"*, which means *"and* **it appears** *that we don't have a room for you tonight."*

So, his language suggested to me that he was not committed to the hotel being full. He may have been lying, or someone else may have told him that the hotel was full and he had no direct knowledge of that himself. He may even have been told to tell me a lie to cover up an error and was uncomfortable with lying. I didn't assume that any one of those alternatives was true. I was fairly certain, however, that I was not being given the facts and that he would not easily retract his stated position.

Approximately 2 minutes later, after a few more questions, I was checked into the penthouse suite at the same hotel, at the cost of a standard room. I recall the conversation well, and used it the next day in the workshop as an example of how to use questions to shift mindsets and negotiate an outcome without accusing people of lying.

My first tack was to direct the discussion back to his hotel and focus on responsibility for the decision. I chose a fairly open question but added some focus and direction by referring to the room that I booked. When reading the questions, think of them being asked quietly, politely.

Q: Oh. What happened to the room I booked?

A: That's been given to someone else.

That question was sufficient, for the time being, to withdraw attention from the Hyatt. However, the manager was good at this game. His answer couldn't get much fuzzier. No one was taking responsibility for selling my room, and if I left it there, I'd be easily guided back to the Hyatt. So I asked a question that would identify how the decision was taken. The more detail I could elicit from the manager, the better quality facts on which I might be able to negotiate a solution if my impression was correct and there may be another room available.

Q: How did that happen?

A: We didn't think you were coming.

Another evasive answer, using the plural 'we', which spreads responsibility for the decision among more than one person without specifying who made the decision. The answer also avoids specifying the conclusion that someone evidently reached to the effect that I was not coming. 'We didn't think you were coming' is once removed from the responsibility of 'We thought you weren't coming', and is typically used to avoid accountability for a decision. In addition, no evidence was offered as a basis for how that decision was reached.

So the next couple of questions are designed to locate accountability and evidence. Notice that each of the questions arises from the previous answer and directs and focuses the manager's awareness on the decision-maker and on the decision process.

Q: Who is 'we'?

A: Me.

Q: (Nods) [pause] *What made you think that I wasn't coming?*

A: You weren't here.

That may be a good reason for selling the room, depending on what time the decision was made, and what notification the manager had available of the time I was due to arrive. No time is specified in his answer, so I needed to know what time frame he was considering, and whether he was aware of my booking notification. The questions are now eliciting specific information, not fuzzy, general information. They are directing the manager's awareness to the issues that enable me to take control of the circumstances, as opposed to the manager controlling the circumstances as he was able to do with his initial fuzzy language.

Q: *What time did you let my room to the other party?*

A: *Around 7:30 p.m.*

Q: *Did you check my booking form to see what time I was due in?*

A: *No.*

Q: *Did you call my mobile phone or home number to see if I was coming?*

A: *No.*

Rather than tell the manager that I'd notified the hotel of my late arrival, or assume that my late arrival time was noted, I opted to go to the best evidence, which would contract, direct and focus awareness on a specific object:

Q: *I wonder could you get my booking form now and let me see it please?*

The reception manager retrieved the booking form, which had my phone numbers and ETA noted as between 9.30 p.m. and 10.00 p.m. The manager had not said that the *only* reason for thinking I was not coming was that I was not there, and as my impression at this stage was that he had tried to avoid responsibility for his decision, I wanted to limit (contract) the possibilities and ensure that there were no other reasons of which I was not aware.

Q: *Apart from the fact that I wasn't here at 7.30 p.m., was there anything else that led you to conclude that I wasn't coming?*

A: *No.*

I was fairly certain that the manager, who by now was far less brazen than when he first spoke, was aware that he had made a mistake. Now it was time to focus on a solution. I chose to let him know that I was not interested in the Hyatt option that night, by making a statement that withdraws from the possibility of the Hyatt, and a question that focuses on the current hotel (nothing against the Hyatt hotels – I often stay at Hyatts).

Q: *Well, I prefer to stay here, where our workshop is being conducted. Do you have any other rooms available?*

A: *No.*

This was a definitive statement, in contrast to his earlier statement that 'It appears that the hotel is full'. I decided to go beyond his assurance and seek evidence. If I needed to, I'd ask to look at the hotel room list, but he might baulk at showing me the list, so I tried another tack first, which directed, focussed and contracted the mind to a specific purpose and action.

Q: *Could you please check whether there are any other rooms available?*

The reception manager went to the computer, scrolled through the data (which I couldn't see), paused at one point, then continued to scroll.

Subtle behaviours such as a sigh, a raised eyebrow or a pause often indicate that something has been considered and then deleted from the mind.

Q: [Observing the pause] *Which room was that?*

A: *It's the penthouse suite, but it's not the type of room that you booked.*

The answer deleted important information, and did not directly answer my previous question. I'd asked if he could check whether any other rooms were available. He did not actually say that the room was available. Based on his answer, the next question filled the gap:

Q: *Is it available?*

A: *Yes.*

Q: *Is that the only room available?*

A: *Yes.*

Q: *What do you think would be the best way to deal with this problem?*

There was no need to criticise the manager or to accuse him of not telling the truth. He offered me the only room available.

Although this example is a customer service matter, the principles embedded in the language and questions are generic. You'll no doubt recognize the forms of the answers from other occasions when you've heard people attempt to avoid being accountable. You'll certainly be more aware of those patterns, and others, as you progress your way through this book.

Review

✓ Fuzzy language is non-specific, general, global, broadly encompassing, often abstract or vague language.

✓ The majority of miscommunication in business arises from the use of fuzzy language.

✓ Accurate communication requires that the speaker and listener, or writer and reader, each has the same internal representation and meaning of the words used.

✓ We filter our raw perceptions through our experiences, attitudes and beliefs to create our reality.

✓ The meaning of your communication is the response that you get.

✓ If you are the listener or reader, the meaning of the communication is the other person's (speaker's or writer's) meaning.

✓ If you want to understand the meaning, it is your responsibility to obtain clarification.

✓ The fuzzometer works on the principle of movements or gaps in awareness. You can enhance and fine tune your 'fuzzometer' by learning to observe what happens to your awareness.

✓ The speaker's language will follow and reflect their processes of awareness.

✓ The listener's awareness will follow the language of the speaker.

✓ The ability to observe your own mind operate is one of the greatest skills a leader can have. It is at the core of the dictum Know Thyself.

✓ Awareness shapes language, language shapes awareness.

✓ A shift in language between specific ◄──────► fuzzy is a clear indicator that questions needed to be asked.

✓ Questions engage the mind.

✓ The processes of consciousness move and shape the mind, its meanings and states of awareness.

✓ Questions activate the processes of consciousness.

✓ The skills of a leader include the skill of shaping human consciousness.

2

Fuzzy Language
Techniques

Chapter 2

FUZZY LANGUAGE TECHNIQUES

There are six common fuzzy language patterns that are used in business:

> **Fuzzy Nouns**
>
> **Fuzzy Verbs**
>
> **Interpretation and Meaning**
>
> **The NOT word**
>
> **Time, Space, Measure**
>
> **Comparators**

Those patterns expand awareness and encompass multiple possibilities.

The questioning techniques that you can use to counter those patterns and clarify the meaning of the fuzzy language are, essentially, questions that contract, direct and focus awareness. Whereas the fuzzy language triggers expanded awareness and global perception or thinking, the questions in this section reverse that process, seek specifics and fill the gaps between the meaning of the language and the internal representation of the listener.

FUZZY NOUNS

Some fuzzy nouns commonly used in business are:

Communication	**Staff**	**Policy**	**Them**
Resources	**Managers**	**Efficiency**	**Us**

A typical example of how a series of fuzzy nouns can be used in a business context is:

> *"We need better communication between staff and managers, and more resources."*

There are at least five fuzzy nouns in that sentence that could be clarified. As a general rule, look for the fuzziest word in the phrase or sentence and clarify that first. In the above example, the most benefit would probably be gained by clarifying the word 'communication', for the following reasons:

- there are probably more means of communication to choose from in the organization than there are resource options (in which case 'communication' is fuzzier than 'resources');

- in that sentence, 'more resources' is an after thought, so it is likely that the communication issue is the dominant issue - people tend to talk first about the issues that dominate their thinking and experience.

- by elucidating what 'communication' means, the speaker will probably also throw light on who 'we' are and which managers and staff are the target of the proposed improved communication.

With nouns, we have several options:

Technique: Clarifying Fuzzy Nouns

1. To define **meaning**:

   "What specifically do you mean by ...?"

2. To identify an **option**:

   "What/which ... specifically?"

3. To identify a **person**:

   "Who specifically do you mean by ...?"

   or

   "Which...(managers etc)...specifically?"

Note that the word 'specifically' is used in each technique. It is possible to use 'exactly' or 'precisely', but generally those words do not elicit the quality of impact of 'specifically'.

The exception is where measurements are involved, and then the words *'precisely'* and *'exactly'* work better than *'specifically'*.

If more than one of those questions is applicable to a particular word, you'll need to decide which question to ask.

Ask yourself *"What would be most useful to deal with – meaning, options or person?"*

In the above example, the following words could be clarified.

1) Who are 'we'?

Does 'we' refer to a group of people, a team, a department, the organization as a whole? The answer will, to a large degree, determine the scale of the problem with communication, and the scale of the solution.

To clarify the first word in the sentence:

We need better communication between staff and managers, and more resources.

the question is simply: *Who, specifically, do you mean by 'we'?*

More often than not, when this question is asked, the answer discloses that the issue is not widespread and that only a few people are concerned about the issue, e.g. communciation in their work area. The word 'we' can make the problem sound bigger than it is, and the problem gets blown out of proportion. There can be a huge difference between the strategies necessary to improve communication among several people and the strategies needed to improve communication across the entire organization. If that issue is not clarified, you could waste a lot of time, money and energy establishing a better way to communicate across the board when the problem is really only local.

This may seem obvious, but such time wastage is a common occurrence. The parties may eventually come to an understanding of how many people are concerned about the issue of communication, but precious time could have been saved by going straight to the point.

Right now, the Quantum Effect is at play. You do not know who is referred to as 'we' in the above example. If you assume (focus on/select) one or other of the potential meanings, your reality will become as you think, and you'll act accordingly. You'll have contracted your awareness of the possibilities to one option by assumption, and you'll gradually build a compelling, concrete reality around that meaning until it becomes a belief and, eventually, the 'fact'. It will remain so until your perception is changed.

However, if you do not make an assumption as to the meaning of a fuzzy word such as 'we', and if you are observing your own awareness, you will notice that there is no concrete meaning in your mind, that your awareness is more expanded in relation to that word, and that several possibilities are suspended in thought awaiting definition.

A similar phenomenon occurs when we hear the phrase 'In Europe'. We then hold a soft focus map or representation of Europe in our awareness, maybe scanning the territory, but never landing, until someone says.....in France. The map of France then becomes clearer as an image. Now we 'know' the meaning of 'In Europe'.

2) '...communication...'

You could ask separately about the meaning of 'better' and 'communication', or clarify their meaning jointly, e.g.

What specifically do you mean by 'better communication'?

By combining the words into a single question the emphasis is then on the difference between quality of communication now and in the future, as opposed to what mode of communication (face to face, email, telephone, meetings), is under review.

However, you'll usually elicit a clearer answer by asking:

What specifically do you mean by communication?

or

What form of communication are you talking about, specifically?

and then asking

What specifically do you mean by 'better'?

The answers should provide you with a clearer understanding, represented by internal images, sounds etc. that correspond to your perceived meaning of what communication looks like (e.g. behaviours), sounds like (e.g. what people are saying) and feels like (e.g. hugging, shaking hands), and what the difference is between the current quality of communication and the desired quality of communication – again in internal visual, auditory and kinesthetic representations.

Notice that the first clarifying question is asked above   in two alternative forms:

What specifically do you mean by communication?

or

What form of communication are you talking about specifically?

The second version of that question varies the form without losing the intention of the first question. It can be monotonous for the speaker and listener to hear the same form of the question "What specifically do you mean by..." too often.

It is important to be able to vary the form when you are asking the same or similar question a number of times in a short period of time. Even changing the location of 'specifically' to the end of the sentence will sound sufficiently different to maintain the listener's interest.

3) '...staff...managers...'

To which staff, and to which managers, does this phrase refer?

For instance, the word 'managers' could be clarifed in several ways:

- what does the speaker mean by 'managers'? They may, for instance, mean supervisors. The distinction between managers and supervisors may be significant in the organization's culture and structure, in which case the question to ask is *'What specifically do you mean by managers?"*

- to which groups of managers is the speaker referring? Is it the managers from X Division, Y Division or both? Is it all managers from that Division or only middle managers? The question to ask is *"Which (group of) managers specifically are you referring to?"*

- who is the speaker referring to – the identity of the managers. The question then is *"Who specifically do you mean by "managers?"*

You may need a combination of those three choices. The decision is situational, whatever is useful for you in the circumstances, e.g.

Q: *What do you mean by 'managers'?*

A: *Supervisors in X Division.*

Q: *Which supervisors specifically?*

A: *The plant supervisors.*

Q: *Who, specifically?*

Notice that each question demands an answer that is more specific than the previous answer. It is a cascade of specificity.

4) '...resources...'

'Resources' is plural form that refers to a class of items. If those items could be different types of item, first ascertain which members of the class are being referred to. In this example, I'll provide answers, to give a better idea of how the questioner must stay present with each answer, and take the meaning deeper.

Q: *Which resources, specifically?*

A: *Money and people.*

Q: *How much money?*

A: *A lot more than we have allocated to this project.*

Q: *Specifically?*

A: *An extra $2 million.*

Q: *And what do you mean by 'people'?*

A: *Competent staff and contractors.*

Q: *Which staff specifically?*

A: Two sales people, 3 admin and 1 project management.

Q: What do you mean by competent?

In that example, the questions probed to a slightly deeper level. In less than a minute, there is enough information to enable you to structure a meaningful discussion, go deeper into the key elements of the issue and get results. The meanings are now much clearer, the beginnings of a potential strategy for solving the issue is being elicited, and the cost of the solution is becoming clearer.

Within those answers are other words that could also be clarified, such as 'What do you mean by admin?' The required administrative person may, for instance, be secretarial or clerical, and once that is clear, the appointment of an admin person can be challenged or planned.

Each question focuses and directs attention or awareness to a particular issue and draws out the details of what the issue looks like, sounds like and feels like (and in some industries such as food and fragrance industries, what it smells and tastes like).

With some further, well-crafted questions, an effective decision can then be made, with increased prospects for success. You might ask about the $2 million - what it is for, how it is calculated, how the figures have been verified, based on estimates or quotes.

You might also test the validity of needing more people – whether the levels of competence described in answer to the last question could be found elsewhere in the organization, whether existing staff and contractors might be able to be trained at less expense than bringing in new staff, whether the need for more people is related to time issues and if it is possible to change roles, duties, priorities and staff allocations in order to free up time using existing resources rather than spend money on recruiting new staff.

It is amazing how a few well-placed questions can reduce potential costs.

It is amazing how a few well-placed questions can reduce potential costs.

Once when I was facilitating a change workshop for a very large company, one of the participants complained that he could not implement the necessary changes in his work area unless he had another $500,000 allocated to his budget. He threatened to leave the change program unless I could get the money for him.

I was a consultant to his company, and, although I had access to the top executive team, I had no input to operational budgets. Besides which, the whole idea of the change workshop was to have people take responsibility for figuring out the answers to their issues, rather than spoon-feeding them.

I asked him if he'd mind giving me some background and then proceeded to ask him some questions - what he would do with the money, which resources he had available now, how those resources were being used, whether they could be re-allocated in a different way, whether there were any frustrating organizational blocks to his section's ability to perform – and in 10 minutes he had outlined a plan that would achieve his result with existing resources plus $10,000. He was delighted, but then I asked how he could juggle his existing budget to ferret out $10,000 from wasted expenditure and apply it to his new plan. In the end, he had the complete solution in less than 15 minutes within his existing budget.

The answers were always there! There was never really 'a problem', other than in the way he was thinking about the issue. The questions that I asked were simple, ordinary questions. However, they were delivered with precision, based on each previous answer, and each question shifted his awareness incrementally until he discovered the solution for himself.

His assertion that he could not implement the changes without $500,000 was global in nature, excluding all other possibilities. He was, effectively, saying "This is impossible unless…". In other words, everything else (high global phrase) will not work, only the $500,000. I then used questions to contract, direct and focus his awareness around the real issues (for which the $500,000 was merely one solution) and then, utilising his own knowledge and skills, asked questions that expanded, re-directed and re-focused his thinking to enable him to create a solution that worked for him and the company.

I recall the circumstances of that incident very well because it was the moment that I realised the significance of two of the key principles that we have since built into in the **MasterProcess** model:

> ➢ **When financial resources are requested, the first solution is usually the more expensive option.**
>
> ➢ **Ask questions to optimise use of the existing resources, and leave the financial resourcing until last. That way, you'll usually save money.**

General rule: Deal with each fuzzy word separately

As a rule of thumb, deal with each noun separately, even if they are related in fact and in the sentence structure, such as 'staff and managers'. If you deal with them together, the other person must answer two questions simultaneously, which will frequently result in

- confusion
- overlooking an important element of the facts
- insufficient sorting of the data
- lack of clarity in the answer.

Each of those factors can be handled by asking some more questions, but it is generally easier, quicker in the long run and more meaningful to allow the person to focus and elaborate on one set of meanings at a time.

Visual or kinesthetic messages

The same questions can be asked in relation to facial expressions, gestures, touching or behaviours.

What did you mean when you raised your eyebrow?

On one occasion, when I was conducting a workshop for lawyers, one of the participants asked me a question about body language. He claimed that if people fold their arms while listening to a presentation, that indicates that they are resisting, or disagreeing with, the message. Although it is important to be aware of postures and gestures - body language – I am wary of interpreting body language according to a formula that predicts its meaning. At that moment there were ten people in the audience of ninety with arms crossed. Lawyers aren't afraid to speak their minds if they disagree, so I asked each of the ten to relate what they were feeling and thinking. All were engaged with, and processing, the content of the workshop, and said they were more relaxed or comfortable with their arms folded.

A similar issue arose with my son, Daniel, when he was about 8 years old. His teacher had told him off for not paying attention in a maths class. I asked Daniel what he was doing at the moment that the teacher asked him to pay attention. He said that he was looking out the window at the side of the classroom. I could understand why the teacher thought he wasn't paying attention. However, I asked Daniel a further question, which went to the meaning of his behaviour: "What do you do when you look out the window?". His answer was "I calculate the answers to the questions the teacher asks." Daniel then explained that he is able to 'see' the figures adding up on an imaginary screen somewhere in the uninterrupted space through the window. He couldn't get a clear screen in his mind when looking at the teacher or when other objects were 'in the way'. I spoke to the teacher the next day and explained what Daniel did. After a pause, he said "That makes sense – Daniel seems to be able to come up with answers quickly without having to write down the figures on paper." From then on the teacher did not interrupt Daniel's window gazing.

It is more useful to ask what behaviour means rather than making assumptions. Quite useful conversations can flow from such questions. They can also remove ambiguity by clarifying intention and thought processes.

Q: *What did you mean when you raised your eyebrow?*

A: *I was surprised by what you said and had some doubts that it is correct.*

Q: *Which part, specifically, do you doubt is correct?*

The conversation can then move towards identifying differences of perception, belief or opinion, and resolving those differences.

Exercise:

From time to time throughout this book you'll see exercises that you can do to practise the techniques.

The techniques are deceptively simple, and you may be tempted to say to yourself "*I know how to do that*" or "*I can do that, I'll skip the exercise*".

I used the term 'deceptively simple' precisely because appearances can be deceiving.

The exercises in this book will assist you to fine tune your ability to know when and how to ask these very ordinary, but nevertheless extraordinary and powerful, questions for greater effectiveness than if you simply read the book and skip the exercises.

Sample answers to each exercise in this book can be viewed at *www.spandah.com/pqfree.htm* or email us at contactus@ spandah.com.

Further listening, reading and awareness exercises and examples are available at that websites to fine tune your skills.

Exercise:

Use each of the three Fuzzy Noun techniques to clarify fuzzy <u>nouns</u> in the following report. Assume that you have been asked to assist with arranging the meeting. Write the full question, including the noun in the space provided:

Executives propose to meet with the other parties in the near future to discuss the implications of the fallout between the project's major partners and the unions. The primary focus will be clarifying the issues that have caused the problems that we are now facing, and how to progress the project so that it works for the parties.

When you've finished that exercise, go back over the questions that you've written and tick off the *one* question that is likely to provide the most useful information.

Cascading meaning

You can ask questions that cascade meaning up or down the specific ◄─────► fuzzy continuum.

You'll find the techniques for cascading up, and expanding awareness, in Chapter 6 (page 209) *The Ripple Effect: Identifying Hidden Meaning, Unstated Purpose and Implications*.

Cascading down by utilising sensory data

Cascading down involves moving the data from general to specific and then to sensory- specific. The senses are a powerful tool for gathering and relaying meaningful information – they are the windows through which we perceive the world and relate to the world.

If you want to get to the facts quickly, and as accurately as possible, target sensory perceptions. The three primary senses for communicating in business are:

Visual	Auditory	Kinesthetic
See	Hear	Feel

In some industries, such as food and fragrance industries, the gustatory (taste) and olfactory (smell) senses have greater prominence in the decision-making process, but generally the visual, auditory and kinesthetic senses are the most dominant in business.

You can elicit a *specific* response by asking a question that requires a *description of sensory data*.

Remember: '*Specific*' requires clearer sensory-specific (*see/hear/ feel*) information, and creates a more contracted/directed/focussed awareness, in which the listener's and speaker's impressions move closer together to a verifiable common meaning.

SPECIFIC =

Visual	Auditory	Kinesthetic
See	Hear	Feel

The question

What specifically do you mean by...?

is one form of question that will obtain a more specific response.

However, if the person being asked the question is in a high 'global' state of mind, and using language that is at the high end of the fuzzy spectrum, you may find that asking that question

- will confuse some people, because it requires a significant shift in restructuring their thought process in order to find the answer; in particular, it requires them to contract their awareness and come down off (literally) a 'high', which can sometimes feel less safe, and less interesting for global thinkers

- may only result in a slightly more specific answer.

Generally I've found it most useful to treat specificity as the objective, and to use the question "What specifically...?" as a half-way station between fuzzy and sensory-specific data. That will almost always make the transition from highly global thinking to sensory specific descriptions smoother and more effective, and at the same time maintain rapport in the interaction, because the transition is more incremental, not sudden, is less confronting and less conspicuous.

It is often useful to elicit and cascade specifics in three stages:

What?	**General/Global**	Bigger Chunks, Expanded
What specifically?	**More Specific**	
See, Hear, Feel?	**Very Specific (Sensory)**	Smaller Chunks, Contracted

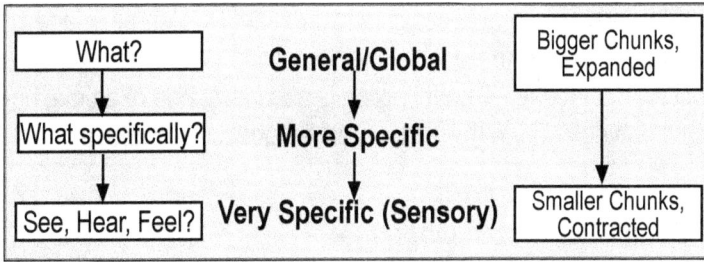

One way to understand the structure of a downward cascade is to answer the question:

What is a part of this?

The more specific data will always be a part of the general description. For instance, consider the phrase "all living things". That is a broad description that requires the mind to expand in order to contemplate it. It is a big chunk of data described in shorthand in three words. By applying the question "What is a part of this?" we can obtain more specific information and descriptions, and at the same time contract, direct and focus awareness:

All living things.

Q: What is a part if 'all living things'?

A: Animal kingdom.

Q: What is a part of the animal kingdom?

A: Mammals

Q: What is a part of the class of mammals?

A: Canines

Q: What is a part of canines?

A: Spaniels

Q: What is a part of the breed spaniels?

A: Cocker spaniels.

Each answer is more specific, and provides a clearer image of the 'living thing'. With each answer the mind is more contracted, directed and focused. The following is a work-related example, but this time I've used the three step cascade described above.

Example: *Global language*:

"We need better communication in our meetings."

General

Q: *What do you mean by better communication?*

A: *'People engaging in discussion more vigorously - vigorous conversations.'*

Specific

Q: *What **specifically** would you hear if there were vigorous discussions?*

A: *'I'd hear people challenging assumptions and beliefs more often, probing the veracity of facts, and looking for ways to improve strategies rather than assuming that what was presented was the best way.'*

More specific, sensory specific

Q: *'What would they be saying/asking. Put it in quotes.'*

A: *'They'd ask: "How do we know that's correct?*

How was the information obtained?

Is there any way of checking it's accuracy?";

and

"Is there another way that we could do this that might be even more effective or that might avoid the risks? How, specifically?"

Notice the difference between the three answers.

Level 1 - General

The question *"What do you mean by better communication"* omits the word 'specifically' and elicits a 'Level 1' general description of the meaning – people engaging in discussions more vigorously, which is a little more specific than 'better communication'. However, although the words 'engaging in' and 'more vigorously' conjure up images of people talking animatedly, you can't 'hear' the specific words, and can only guess at what the other person imagines how they are behaving and what they are saying.

Level 2 - Specific

The next question, *"What **specifically** would you hear if there were vigorous conversations"*, takes the meaning of 'better communication' to Level 2 of clarity and meaning – it directs attention to the auditory components of 'more vigorous discussions'. The answer:

> *"I'd hear people challenging assumptions and beliefs more often, probing the veracity of facts, and looking for ways to improve strategies rather than assuming that what was presented was the best way."*

provides *descriptions of* what people would be saying -
probing the veracity of facts, challenging assumptions - and is therefore more specific than 'engaging in more vigorous discussions' because it tells you something about what the person means by 'vigorous discussions'.

You may have noticed something else – the question was phrased to obtain the auditory data by asking *"What would you **hear**..."*. So the question is already tapping into the auditory sense, which in this example is the dominant and relevant sense. But is the information sensory-specific?

No. It is still *an interpretation of* the sensory data. It does not give you the actual sensory data. It only gives you the person's interpretation of the sensory information that they would see and hear.

Make a note of this next point:

> **Most people will stop at Level 2, which is a description of (or 'talking about') something that was experienced, seen, felt, or heard.**
>
> **The key to understanding the facts is to go further, to Level 3, to what actually occurred, what was actually seen, heard or felt.**

Level 3 – Sensory specific

The question at Level 3 demands the most specific information. It requires a description of the actual events as perceived. In this example it asks for that information by asking *"What would they be saying/asking. Put it in quotes."*

The request to *'put it in quotes'* requires the person to repeat what they *actually* heard, and enables the listener to directly assess the meaning of the words quoted, without interpretation or filtering. In other words, you get the raw, sensory data.

In that example, the sensory-specific information is the words/sounds that would be heard *as if you are actually witnessing a conversation.*

> ## General rule:
> **When what was said may be important, ask for the conversation to be described in quotes.**
>
> **If the person says "I don't recall exactly", simply say "As best you can recall".**

In 99% of cases, the Level 3 description of the conversation in quotes will be significantly different and more accurate than the description at Level 2.

The phrase 'better communication' is global, and means very little, in the sense that it is very difficult to ascribe a sensible meaning to it without having more information, whereas the last answer provides a model and process for making 'better communication' work.

Notice that you can elicit the sensory data with a question in the form:

What did/would you actually see/hear/feel?

However, it is best not to ask for data on all three senses in one question, as it will be difficult for the person to process information in all three modalities (visual, auditory, kinesthetic) simultaneously. Instead, split the senses into separate questions and obtain the answer to one sense before you ask the question on the next sense:

What did you actually see?

What did you actually hear?

What did you actually feel?

and, for future descriptions

What would you actually see?

What would you actually hear?

What would you actually feel?

I cannot begin to tell you how often I've heard Level 3 sensory data uncover the true facts, potential risks and potential solutions in business. It's where you witness the difference between fact and interpretation/assumption/opinion.

Selecting the most useful words to clarify

The art of using the **Powerful Questions** is to select those words or phrases in a sentence or paragraph which, when clarified, will produce the most useful outcome. That will depend to some degree on the context of the conversation and on how much the listener knows about the situation.

If you ask questions about every fuzzy word in every sentence, the conversation won't go far, and will quickly get bogged down in *minutae*.

It is helpful to apply the *Pareto (80/20)* principle:

**Which 20% of fuzzy language will,
when clarified, give you 80% of the meaning
that will lead to a result?**

Your particular interest in the subject-matter and the context of the discussion will have a strong influence on which words you choose to clarify.

As a rule of thumb, listen for the fuzziest word or phrase, the words that have least meaning for you, or the words that expand your awareness the most in a sentence, and ask clarifying questions about them first.

That is a listening and awareness skill that can be learned after only a short period of practice.

Make sure that you ask the question soon after hearing the word or phrase that you want to clarify. The longer you leave it, the more likely that a belated question will cause confusion. I might ask a question within a few seconds after hearing a fuzzy word that I want to have clarified, or I may listen to what amounts to a whole paragraph, before asking the question. I 'mentally tag' the fuzzy words and phrases in my memory and assess which words or phrases will be most useful to clarify. If the later part of a sentence or paragraph makes sense of the word that I selected, I scan for another word or phrase that needs clarification.

When I am talking to someone on the phone, I often jot down the key words and phrases that I want to know more about.

When you are unsure of which word to question, clarify more than one. Generally, the first answer you receive will give you a good indication of whether another question about the same noun needs to be asked. If the answer is very specific, that may be sufficient; if the answer is only slightly less fuzzy, you may need to clarify the meaning further.

In most cases the questions and answers will take only a few seconds of time. This is where a stitch in time saves nine. It is better to ask a question and be sure that your understanding is clear than to assume that you know what the person means and find out later that you are on different tracks.

FUZZY VERBS

Fuzzy nouns and fuzzy verbs are the most common language patterns that require clarification.

Fuzzy verbs include 'doing' words such as:

Prepare	**Make**	**Write**	**Present**	**Ask**
Do	**Instruct**	**Delegate**	**Organise**	**Plan**

Verbs are shorthand descriptions for an action or a series of actions. Their *'fuzzy'* nature arises not only from the meaning of the verb, but also the number of ways in which the action can be executed.

Example:
"I'd suggest we let the audit committee handle this."

In this example, the word 'handle' is unclear in two respects – what the word means and to what process the word refers. The question that elicits process is dealt with later in this book. For the moment we'll look at how to identify the meaning of the verb.

The technique is the same as one of the techniques for clarifying nouns:

Example:

Technique: Clarifying Fuzzy Verbs

To identify the *meaning*:
"What specifically do you mean by ...?"

What, specifically, do you mean by "handle"?

In this example, the speaker may mean fix, investigate, get rid of, cover up, etc, each of which will have many options for implementation (process), and some of which may not be ethically acceptable to an organisation. You'll only know that it is ethically unacceptable if you ask the question and find out what the word 'handle' means.

It's easy to imagine that some of the professional services firms that have, in recent years, been fined for destroying documents relevant to corporate frauds may have had a meeting at which someone said 'Let me handle this', and that nobody asked what that meant, possibly because they didn't want to know, but perhaps because they assumed that the matter would be handled legally.

This raises an important point – our values and ethics will often dictate whether we ask a 'hard' question. Our choices will, in turn, impact on the corporate awareness, and will be reflected in the corporate culture. Culture is determined by our choices of thinking and behaviour. Culture can be changed at any time by changing our thinking and behaviour.

Take two minutes to complete the exercise on the next page.

Exercise:

Use the Clarifying Fuzzy Verbs technique to clarify the fuzzy verbs in the following report. It is the same paragraph that you worked on with fuzzy noun techniques, except that now you look for the fuzzy verbs. Continue to assume that you have been asked to assist with arranging the meeting. Write the full question, including the verb:

Executives propose to meet with the other parties in the near future to discuss the implications of the fallout between the major partners to the project and the unions. The primary focus will be clarifying the issues between them that have caused the problems that we are now facing, and how to progress the project so that it works for all parties.

When you have written the questions down, prioritise the questions according to the value of the information that they are likely to elicit.

The question *"What specifically do you mean by 'propose'?"* will probably elicit what the executives said about their intention to meet, and may also identify the process by which the proposal will be made, e.g.:

> *"They thought it was appropriate for the CEO to take the initiative and invite the CEOs of the project partners and the union Presidents to meet in two weeks' time at a neutral venue to discuss the problems."*

If you wanted more information about the executives' thought processes around the approach to the other parties, you could cascade down to sensory data:

Q: *What, specifically, did they say about the proposal to meet?*

A: *The CEO preferred to write to each party and outline what we have in mind. Janet suggested that the CEO call each of his counterparts and chat to them personally. She thought that he could perhaps gauge their general feelings about the issues that way, so that we could better anticipate the mood and positions at the meeting. Bill suggested that we hold the meeting on our company yacht so that they couldn't walk away, but most felt that a CBD hotel would be the best venue."*

The question *"What specifically do you mean by 'discuss'?"* will elicit some detail about the the proposed process for discussion:

> *They didn't suggest any specific way of conducting the discussions. The CEO thought that it would be best to ask the people he's inviting how they'd like to conduct the meeting. The others thought that you might come up with some ideas about how to structure the meeting, and what processes to use.*

If you ask about the verbs 'clarifying', 'progress' and 'works', you'll probably find it useful to cascade to Level 3 and obtain sensory-specific data:

> *What would we see/hear if the issues were clarified to the degree that is useful for the parties?*
>
> *What would be sufficient progress? What would we see happening that's not happening now?"*
>
> *How would we know that it's working for us?*

The answers to those questions will provide the outcomes that your executives want from the meeting, which in turn will influence the process that you design for the meeting. If the executive team did not discuss those points, or the person briefing you does not know their thoughts, you'll know that there is some missing information that may be helpful in designing the meeting. Those questions may also be useful to pose to the CEO's counterparts in the partners and unions prior to, or at the commencement of, the meeting.

Notice that you don't have to work out the answers yourself. You simply need to listen, and work with the other person moment by moment using their language as a guide to obtain a clearer understanding of their reality. This last point is important. It means that you must stay 'present' with the other person.

INTERPRETATIONS AND CONCLUSIONS

Some fuzzy language is in fact an interpretation or conclusion ascribed by a person to a particular situation, e.g.

"This is a difficult job."

or

"The client responded negatively to our suggestion."

What is difficult or negative for one person is not necessarily so for another. Those words have a subjective, contextual meaning and truth, not an absolute meaning.

To deal with this type of language, first ascertain meaning, and then the facts (sensory data - what was seen, felt, heard) so that the interpretation is removed.

Fuzzy words	Clarify
This is a difficult job	**What do you mean by difficult?** **Which part specifically do you find difficult?**
The clients responded negatively	*What do you mean by negatively?* *What did they say? Specifically?* *Can you put their words in quotes?*
They didn't like it	**What didn't they like?** **What specifically did they say?** **Put their words in quotes (as best you can).**
It'll fail	*What do you mean by fail?* *Which part specifically do you think will fail?*

General rules for handling interpretation:

1) *Clarify 'What...' first, then 'How...'.*

This is a basic rule for using the **Powerful Questions** generally, not only for interpretations. First clarify the meaning of the word or phrase and then identify the process.

What ────► How

Once you clarify the meaning of the words, it is easier to do something useful with it, using a process ('how') question. For instance:

What do you mean by difficult?

Which part of the job specifically do you find difficult?

How are you doing that?

How could you do that in an easier way?

Who might be able to show you an easier way to do that?

Notice that the third question inquires about the current process, and the fourth and fifth questions in that sequence shift into solutions (how to improve the process). Those questions are designed to empower the person who has the issue to figure out their own solution.

You could, of course, demonstrate how the task could be done, or tell them how to do things differently – either may be appropriate depending on the circumstances, but it is worth bearing in mind an ancient and universal truth that is stated simply in the *Tao Te Ching:*

**As interfering help is given,
ability and confidence are taken away.**

Another example might be:

What do you mean by 'the client responded negatively'?

What specifically did they say?

How can we salvage the contract, keep the client happy and still make a profit on the deal?

How, specifically, would we do that?

2) *If the description has multiple components, identify the part where the issue arises:*

When the description refers to a complex item, a process or strategy, ask *"Which part...":*

What do you mean by fail?

Which part specifically do you think will fail?

How do you think that would happen?

How do you know that would happen?

How could we do it to ensure that it will work?

3) *Third party responses:*

Where someone has given a response (verbal or behavioural) that is the subject of interpretation, obtain the sensory data that specifically describes the response:

What was it about the offer that they didn't like?

What specifically did they say?

How can we make the deal more attractive to them?

The NOT word

When someone describes a situation in terms of what is not, they often also delete vital information as to what is.

Examples:

The result wasn't acceptable to them.

The submission was not to specification.

The accounting procedures didn't comply with statutory requirements.

The revenue doesn't match forecasts.

They didn't follow instructions properly.

We didn't present the information as well as we could have.

In many cases there will follow a clear explanation of what was required and solutions for dealing with the problem, which is tempting to accept.

However, the fact that an explanation and solution is given does not mean that the issue has been dealt with properly – it could be a tactic of 'confession and avoidance', designed to take the heat off the person making the confession. For instance, Bob tells you:

"The contractors didn't follow instructions properly. But it's been handled - I've spoken to them and made it clear how we want the job done. They understand, and will be rectifying the work tomorrow."

Bob has squarely placed the blame on the contractors. Is there a possibility here that Bob is deflecting attention from his own error? What if Bob gave the wrong instructions, omitted to give full instructions or gave ambiguous instructions? If Bob is avoiding responsibility for his part in giving the instructions, is it possible that Bob may not actually know how to give clear instructions and may repeat the error in future? If that is the case, and you 'buy' Bob's explanation, what degree of responsibility falls on your shoulders if the error is repeated on a later project?

How will you handle Bob's explanation? Would you handle it any differently if tomorrow is the very last day for getting the work to schedule, otherwise your company will incur significant losses? Would you handle it any differently if this were the third occasion where the same thing and same explanation has occurred, all involving Bob?

In addition, does what Bob said provide you with a clear understanding of what he has now instructed the contractor and whether the rectification activities will work? What if there is a better way to carry out the rectification work that perhaps Bob and the contractor haven't considered? Would you be concerned about being accused of micro-managing Bob?

If Bob has, in fact, screwed up and you don't probe a little more into what he said, you may be missing an excellent opportunity to coach Bob to improve his skills and performance, as well as to ensure that the company's interests are taken care of.

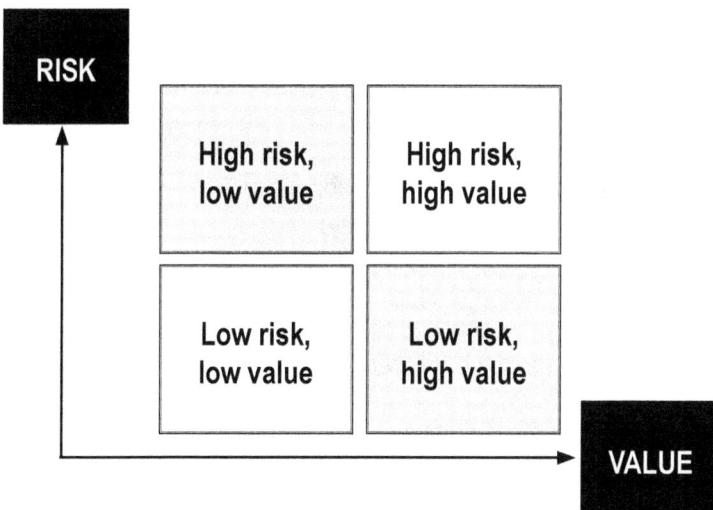

RISK

	High risk, low value	High risk, high value
	Low risk, low value	Low risk, high value

VALUE

Many business leaders will not intervene unless the issue is on the right hand side of the risk/value matrix – high risk and high value or low risk and high value.

However, organisations which have a coaching culture tend to look to the more numerous opportunities created by high risk/low value and low risk/low value circumstances to coach their people in skills that will be useful in high value situations. Those opportunities are not looked on as interference or micro-management, but as occasions where the person being coached can learn skills and values without pressure. Usually only a couple of coaching sessions are needed for the learnings to be assimilated and from there onwards risk is reduced and less intervention is required. Perhaps the most important lesson and value is self-honesty and to deal with any problems openly and effectively.

The following technique will assist you:

Technique:
The NOT word

1 Ascertain specifics of what 'ought' to have been, and the basis for that position
   (if not self-evident, such as with legislative requirements)

2 Ascertain what actually happened, what are the facts (sensory)

3 Identify the difference

4 Identify how the difference occurred

5 Identify a solution/course of action.

Example: *The results are not in line with forecast.*

1 *What, specifically was the forecast?*

   What were the facts and assumptions on which we based the forecast?

   Were/are the facts and assumptions valid?

2 *What is the actual result?*

   How do we know that?

3 *What, specifically is the discrepancy?*

   How do we know that?

4 *How did the difference occur?*

   How, specifically, was that done?

5 *How do we remedy the situation / make up the difference?*

   Knowing what we know now, is there a better way to do it so that we can exceed forecast?

Using that model, the conversation with Bob might go like this:

   "The contractors didn't follow instructions properly. But it's been handled – I've spoken to them and made it clear how we want the job done. They understand, and will be rectifying the work tomorrow."

1) Ascertain specifics of what 'ought' to have been, and the basis for that position

Q: *What should they have done that they didn't do?*

A: *They should have factored all the payment variations into the new software system so that the program would handle all of the different supplier payment terms.*

Q: How many different payment structures have to be factored in?

A: Eight

Q: How do we know that the contractors were supposed to do that?

A: The contract requires them to provide a payment system for the whole company. It's implicit that they have to take account of all the supplier payment structures and variations.

Q: [Not prepared to rely on an interpretation of the contract that is 'implicit'] Show me the contract terms.

2) Ascertain what actually happened, what are the facts (sensory).

Q: So what did they do?

A: They included all eight of the standard payment structures but did not take account of the extent to which accounts staff resolved individual supplier issues and local arrangements by turning off the previous software and processing the data manually.

Q: What did the contractors actually do instead?

A: They simply entered details of standard payment structures without the local variations.

3) Identify the difference

Q: So the difference between what ought to have been done and what was done is that the non-standard local variations that have been relied on and entered manually in the past were not built into the system?

A: Yes.

4) Identify how the difference occurred

Q: *How did that happen?*

A: *The contractors did not gather all the necessary information.*

Q: *How did they gather the information about our procedures?*

A: *They asked our accounts department.*

Q: *What information did the accounts department give them?*

A: *The standard payment structures.*

Q: *And the local variations?*

A: *No. The variations have never been recorded. They are something that the accounts people at each location do as and when required.*

Q: *So the contractors were not made aware of the local variations?*

A: *That's correct.*

5) Identify a solution/course of action.

Q: *How is this being resolved?*

A: *I've instructed the contractors to modify the program to account for all the variations and ensure that the whole system is operational.*

Q: *How, specifically, will they know what those variations are?*

A: *All relevant staff who have been manually entering the variable data met today with the contractors and gave detailed step-by-step processes for the variations.*

Q: *How many staff?*

A: Six. The remainder adhered to the standard payment system.

Q: How will the contractors be carrying out your instructions?

A: The first step was today, obtaining details of the variations. They will now design software changes and enter data to accommodate the variations. Each variation will be tested individually to ensure that all elements of the program work before going live.

Q: When, specifically, will the work be completed and the system up and running correctly?

A: By close of business Friday next week.

Q: Please report to me at the end of each day by email with the specifics of what has been done, the results and progress, any problems or delays and what will be done to overcome the delays or problems.

A: OK.

Q: It seems to me that the problem was not created by the contractor, but by us. What are you doing to ensure that the same or similar problem does not occur in future on software system changes or changes to other systems?

There are obviously other questions and issues that might be raised in this example, such as whether to allow variations from the standard system. However, the point of the exercise is to demonstrate how a few well-placed questions can hold Bob accountable for improving the company's systems, rather than allowing him to blame contractors and avoiding responsibility.

Exercise:

Which questions would you ask to deal with the following statement?

'*The submission was not to specification.*'

1   Ascertain specifics of what 'ought' to have been, and the basis for that position

2   Ascertain what actually happened, what are the facts (sensory)

3   Identify the difference

4   Identify how the difference occurred

5   Identify a solution/course of action

There is also a short version of the '*not*' word technique, that uses the word 'instead'.

That was used in Step 2 of the previous example:

Q: What did the contractors actually do instead?

For instance:

• *Many issues initially were not well described.*

Q: How were they described, instead?

- *Without that support, the project would not have progressed as far and as fast as it did.*

  Q: *How far would it have progressed, instead?*

- *What was not understood and appreciated was...*

  Q: *What was understood, instead?*

- *These cases were not always reported.*

  Q: *What was done with those cases, instead?*

In many cases, the short form questions will identify a failure in systems or process that can be readily recitified by a couple of further questions:

These cases were not always reported.

  Q: *What was done with those cases, instead?*

  Q: *What was it about the reporting system that enabled those cases to slip through without being reported?*

  Q: *How can we improve the system so that it captures those cases?*

By now, you'll probably realise that I am a big fan of asking follow-up questions along the lines of 'How can we improve the current situation?'. It is tragic how often that question is overlooked. It can be asked when something hasn't worked as well as you'd like, and can also be asked when things are going well. Whatever you are doing, there is usually a way to improve it. If you don't, someone else will, eventually.

Time, Space, Measure

Issues relating to time, space and measure frequently blend into our business conversations when outcomes are relevant, which is most of the time.

Very few business discussions can be completed without reference to 'when', 'where' or 'how many' - time, space and measure.

When outcomes are discussed, the language used is generally fairly specific, particularly towards the end of a discussion when action steps are mentioned. However, fuzzier language is often found in the early part of conversations, meetings and negotiations, especially where someone is attempting to provide a summary of events, hide information, avoid responsibility or exaggerate circumstances.

When fuzzy language is used to describe time, space, distance, volume or weight, fuzzy words expand awareness, soften focus and/or generalise location, direction, time and measure. The general technique to deal with them is to ask for specifics:

	Words & Phrases	Technique
Time	Recently	When, specifically?
	Last week	When, specifically? Which day?
	Lengthy wait	How long, specifically?
	Soon	When, specifically?
	As soon as possible	When, specifically?
	Later today	What time?
Space	Worldwide	Which countries, specifically?
	In the UK	Where, specifically, in the UK?
	Close by/near	How far, specifically?
		Which direction, specifically?
	Above/below	Where, specifically?
Measure	A lot / many	How many, specifically?
	More	How much (more), specifically?
	Bigger	How big/much bigger, specifically?
	Long	How long, specifically?
	Extensive	How extensive, specifically?
	Considerable	How much is 'considerable'?
		How much, specifically?

If you hear those words at the completion of a negotiation, clarify the speaker's meaning immediately.

You may choose to cascade the meaning from level 1 to level 3:

"There's a lengthy wait."

Level 1 *"How long?"*

"Months."

Level 2 *"How many months specifically?"*

"Two."

Level 3 *"So when will it be delivered? Give me a firm date."*

"March 26th."

March 26th is sensory-specific because it can be seen on the calendar and is a defined date.

Exercise: Clarify the time, space and measure language in the following using the above techniques:

Recent hurricanes in the USA impacted fuel supplies and prices worldwide. Many drivers found themselves in long queues with a lengthy wait to fill up at the bowser. The fuel prices are predicted to get a lot higher in coming weeks, which is causing considerable concern to the average family, which does not have much room in the family budget to absorb these extensive price rises.

Consider the following extract from a report presented to an executive committee, and notice how the use of time, space and measure language avoids accountability. And yes, this is from an actual report to the executives of a real company.

Trends:

The number of estimates received has *increased significantly*, particularly in the area of engineering projects. We believe that this trend should transfer into *won projects* in the next *four to six* weeks.

Contracts:

Major ongoing contracts are as follows:

Project 1: As reported in the last meeting this contract has lost *substantial* sums of money.

Project 2: This contract is proceeding *on budget* but *behind time* due to wet weather. We have had *a number* of *minor* accidents on site which has resulted in *a flurry* of paperwork. A QA audit carried out a week ago has brought *additional* work as our QA has to be updated.

Project 3: - should be completed *within two weeks*.

Project 4: – will finish *within two weeks*.

Project 5: is not profitable as it was *underestimated*. Traffic management costs have *blown out*. Project has $110K of remaining works to be completed. These works were *delayed* due to problems with the government diverting traffic flow.

Project 6: Client requires us to complete the final works *before* we receive the remainder of our claim. This should occur *within three weeks*.

New Work:

The number of projects offered to us for tendering *has increased* and we have won *several*, and are on the *short list* for others. Our problem is that *some* of these jobs are now *delayed until after* New Year.

Estimating:

We have registered 105 tenders but *a lot of* projects have been *delayed* for *numerous reasons*. Presently both Don and Martin are fielding *a lot of* enquiries for remediation work from clients. It appears that if we are successful in winning these projects we have a very busy *period after* the New Year break. We are *short listed* for *a number of projects* that should commence *shortly*.

I have italicised the relevant words that have time/space/measure elements. Names, industry and other features that might identify the company have been changed, as is the case with other examples throughout the book, unless otherwise stated.

You'll possibly have noticed that the author of the report also uses fudging words such as 'should be' and 'it appears', which are often used in conjunction with fuzzy time, space and measure language.

Problems with time and space

Time and space are concepts that we have created to enable us to make sense of the three dimensional world. Our consciousness is not limited by time and space, but the way we conceptualise time and space can severely restrict our ability to operate at optimal levels in business.

We often use the language of time and space to limit and define our actions and options. Let me give two examples, both of which occurred during change workshops in which I was facilitating the participants to solve problems of innovation that they thought were difficult or impossible, or to create something that was not presently possible. You'll notice how the initial issue and answers indirectly referred to time and space/place, and how questions can quickly clarify issues and open up opportunities, with all the solutions (and ownership of the solutions) emanating from the person with the problem.

Example 1: Space/place

> *We have an idea for modifying a telecommunications device, but we haven't been able to find the answer to a technical problem. We've tried everything we can think of and nothing worked. We have now hit a brick wall.*

In this statement 'we haven't been able to find the answer' and 'we've tried everything we can think of' suggest that there is a group of people who have limited the search for the answer to themselves. Knowing who they are will probably define their parameters and, therefore, their 'space' limits.

There is almost certainly a contraction or limitation of awareness in that statement, and certainly a contraction of the 'search' function of consciousness. I have included comments that reflect my thought process as I asked the following questions.

Q: *Who is 'we'?*

A: *Me and my team.*

The search was probably limited to within the company but I'll check anyway. I'll use an open question, not a closed question that assumes that they have only looked within their company, such as 'Do you mean you and your team in the company?'. If they have only sought the answers within the company, that will become evident from the answer to the open question. If they have looked outside their company, my assumption is incorrect and the 'space' issue is broader than I'd thought. Notice that the closed question contracts awareness and gives a narrow focus to the answer. The open question expands awareness, and makes no assumptions.

Q: *Where have you looked for the solution?*

A: *Everywhere we can in the company.*

For some reason the team's awareness is limited to the company they work for. The next question checks whether that is correct.

Q: *Have you looked outside the company?*

A: *No.*

I rarely ask 'why' or 'why not', because they often only lead to excuses and blame, but in this instance I wanted to identify any limiting belief that was behind their choice not to look outside the company. The belief will give a clue about how to frame the next question.

Q: *Why not?*

A: *We are the biggest in the country in this industry and if we don't have the answer, no one else will.*

Now we have identified the geographical (space/place) boundary. The search for an answer is limited to the country, not just the company. You could challenge that belief, but there is no need to spend the energy and time doing that. The key here is to expand the person's awareness and direct and focus it to another place where the answer may be. A safe assumption is that there is someone, somewhere in the world, who may have some information that will help. I need to ask a question that expands awareness, re-directs attention away (withdraws) from the limitation and creates (emanates) another possibility. Notice that the next question is intentionally full of fuzzy language that instructs the mind to move freely/expand. I used that language because we have to contend with the belief that if this company doesn't know the answer, then no one else will know (a belief that results from contracted awareness). I choose language and frames of reference designed to expand awareness in a way that is virtually impossible to deny. All I want to do is create a crack in the limiting belief, and then we can move forward:

Q: *Is it possible that there may be someone, somewhere in the world who may have been doing research or development work in this area and who may have some ideas or knowledge that might be useful in this situation?*

A: *I guess so.*

That answer is non-committal, probably because the person does not know anyone, or recall anyone of that description. However, their mind has now moved at least partly out of the self-imposed limitation. The next question takes their mind further in that direction. It assumes that such a person exists and directs and focuses the mind towards a specific location. If they answer this question, they will be moving towards a solution.

Q: *If there were such a person, where do you think they might be?*

A: *Perhaps Japan. Or maybe the U.S.*

That answer creates two options. You can go with either or both options, but the easiest way is to draw on the person's own industry knowledge and ask the person to nominate which of the two is the stronger option. You can always come back to the second option later if the first option does not bear fruit. The idea here is to target the most workable solution.

Q: *Which of those is most likely?*

A: *The U.S.*

Now I'll focus on eliciting a more defined region of the U.S., with a question that contracts, directs and focuses awareness.

Q: *Where in the U.S. do you think they might be located?*

A: *Probably California.*

In giving that answer the person is processing information that they may not consciously recall. You could ask 'Where, specifically in California?' but the previous answer stated 'probably California', which suggests that the person is uncertain. Asking for specific cities etc. risks drawing a blank, disengagement and loss of rapport. The next question switched track to finding the specific location, as opposed to recalling the location. Again, using fuzzy language to open up possibilities.

Q: *How do you think you might be able to locate them?*

A: *[Pause] Well, now that I think about it, I read about some similar research in a technical journal last year. I could contact them through the journal article.*

This information is more concrete, so the search now switches to finding the journal that will lead to the relevant person and information.

Q: *Where can you get a copy of the journal article?*

A: *It's in my office among a pile of journals on the floor.*

At the next break, the participant telephoned the journal, located the writer of the article and obtained information about how to resolve the problem.

There was, in fact, never a problem. The answer was always there, but the person's process for finding the solution was lacking.

Example 2: Time

> *We've come up with a groundbreaking idea, but what we want to do is too advanced. We simply don't have the technology or science to do what would be required.*

This statement denies the person's ability to do what is required. The words 'too advanced' and 'simply don't have' refer to time, and contract awareness to the present knowledge, science and technology whilst extending the denial of ability into the future. When you hear this type of language, the sub-text is something like 'and I can't see us developing that knowledge in the foreseeable future' . The physical universe may appear to have time frames, but consiousness has no such limitation unless we believe the limitation is real.   The first question withdraws that limitation.

> *Q: ...Yet?*
>   *(i.e. 'You don't have the technology or science...yet?')*

> *A: Yes.*

They don't have the science or technology at the moment, and there the limitation ends. Implicit in the answer is that we might discover the science and technology sometime in the future. Instead of closing down the possibility, the question has opened the door to find what they need. Now we only need to step through the door and abridge the time frame.

> *Q: When do you think it is likely that the technology and science will be available?*

> *A: Oh, a long while away.*

Q: How long, specifically?

A: Oh, I don't know.

The next question does not ask for specifics, because the person has denied knowledge. Instead, the question asks for an estimate, but still gives direction and expands awareness.

Q: Ball park?

A: [Shakes head, then says] Maybe 20 or 30 years.

The 'maybe' is non-committal, and the time frame covers a 10 year period. There is a good chance that a longer time frame will elicit greater certainty. The next question expands awareness.

Q: What about in 100 years?

A: [Slightly bemused] Oh, sure. They'd probably be well beyond that technology by then.

Somewhere in the person's consciousness is the information that suggests that a solution will exist in 100 years' time, which is consistent with the initial statement that the idea is 'too advanced'. The person is not yet consciously aware of that information, which is perhaps a floating possibility awaiting human consciousness to attract it, as with the Quantum Effect principle. The next task is to ask a question that directs the person's awareness to that information:

Q: And how do you think they'd put it together in 100 years' time?

The participant then described a future solution, all of which was actually flowing from his own consciousness. Having identified the idea, the following questions will focus on the immediate future and concrete actions and present time, giving a sense of empowerment.

> Q: *Good. Now, which three things would you need to do to start developing that solution?*

The participant described several steps.

> Q: *When could you commence those steps?*
>
> A: *Any time.*

The solution is no longer out of reach, but we still need to bring the time frame to a manageable level and ensure that his belief about the viability of the idea is positive.

> Q: *If you were to commence those steps tomorrow, and put the necessary resources behind the initiative, how long do you think it would take to develop the solution?*
>
> A: *[Pause] About 5 years.*

The issue was never about science and technology, but always about how to expand beyond the current beliefs and perceptions and tap into a deeper awareness. The entire process took only a few minutes. The *'impossible'* problem had now become an opportunity.

COMPARATORS

Comparators include words such as:

Better	**Best**	**Bigger**	**Biggest**
More	**Most**	**Faster**	**Fastest**
Longer	**Longest**	**Higher**	**Highest**

All of these words compare X with Y. Often people will simply use those words without stating what is being compared, in which case potentially useful information is missing:

We want better conditions.

We are planning to grab a bigger share of the market.

This is a faster track to profitability.

If the comparison is not made explicit, you will have to make an assumption about what the other person means, or clarify their meaning.

You can always ask *"What do you mean by better/bigger/faster?"* but that question will often elicit a description of the end outcome, such as a list of the desired conditions, or what slice of market share is contemplated. The question doesn't tell you what is driving the idea. It is often useful to ask that question after either of the following questions:

Technique: Comparators

"... than what?"

or

"...compared to what?"

Example:

"Bigger compared to what?"

"Better than what?"

You'll then have a better idea of what the other person's frame of thinking and motivation is - and it may not be what you thought it would be.

It is quite a different proposition to mean *"We are planning to grab a bigger share of the market compared to our major competitor"* as opposed to *"We are planning to grab a bigger share of the market than we have now."* The latter may only require an incremental increase to be successful, whereas the former may require substantial resources and a substantially different strategy, because you may have to compete on another organisation's terms. In either case, you can follow up with *"How much bigger?"* or *"How big specifically?"* to ascertain the dimensions of the change.

Ask for specifics

When you are clear about what is being compared, ask for the specific measure eg:

How long, specifically?

How much bigger?

How much more, specifically?

SOFTENERS – the Columbo method

You will obtain a better outcome in any communication if you build and hold rapport with the other person. Rapport skills include the ability to formulate a question to obtain the outcome that is most useful, and to maintain rapport and co-operation while asking challenging questions. The manner in which the questions are asked will impact substantially on the outcome of the interaction.

A *'softener'* is a way of leading into a question that prepares the other person for the question and justifies the asking of the question.

We call this *'the Columbo method'* after the TV detective of the same name. Detective Columbo, played by Peter Falk, had a trademark habit of asking an important question as if it was an afterthought, with a preface *"There's just one thing that I don't understand. Perhaps you can help me..."* or (as he turns while walking toward the door) *"Just one more thing. I was wondering...."*.

'Softeners' lower resistance and enable you to maintain rapport whilst challenging the other person to be more specific.

Softeners

"I'm wondering...... "   "It would help me if..... "

"I need to get a clear picture....... "   "I'm curious...... "

"Could you tell me...... "   "I'm not clear on something....."

"I'm not sure I understand. Can you show/explain/outline..."

Notice that all of the softeners refer to "I", and do not blame the other person for mis-communication. They ask for help from the other person.

However, your question after the softener should guide the other person's mind to the issue that requires clarification and to a process that will lead to, or create, a workable outcome:

Examples:

> *"I'm not sure I understand. Can you outline how, specifically, we could do that successfully, especially in view of the client's adverse feedback?"*

> *"I'm not clear on something. It would help me if you could explain the planning process and where, specifically, our thinking or actions did not work when drawing up the plan."*

> *"I know that we have egg on our faces because of this debacle, and we've been over the system failures in detail. What would be helpful for me at this stage is to consider what, specifically, we have learned from these events about our systems and the way we - as a Board and as individuals - dealt with this whole matter and how, specifically, we will deal with these issues in future so that we have a successful outcome.*

> *"I was just wondering – it wasn't clear to me in the presentation – how, specifically will this approach deal with the recent legislative changes and how do we know that it will work?"*

Notice that the questions   partially direct and focus the other person's awareness - in these instances towards overcoming a potential weakness in a proposal or to a weakness in the planning process, and in the third example towards personal and Board performance and process. The focus is on what can be learned and how to do things in a way that will work. Make that a framework of your questions where possible.

Managing a meeting

If you are asking the questions as part of a Board, executive or management team, or other team within an organisation or in a project, it is very helpful for all (or at least some) of the other team members to also be familiar with the **Powerful Questions**, otherwise you'll find that others on the team may not understand the nature, effect or sequence of questions and may interrupt and 'lose' the process. If they understand the process and questions, you'll be able to get to the point and outcome quicker, with less effort and with their support

However, when you are the only person on the team who knows the **Powerful Questions** techniques, you may have to manage interruptions by using a softener and setting a framework for what you are about to ask, e.g.

> *I'm not sure that I understand what happened or how the remedial strategy will work and I have four or five questions in relation to this matter*

so that the others in the group are aware that you'll be asking more than one question, and are less likely to interrupt.

Application to NAB report

Exercise:

Before we leave the topic of fuzzy language, consider the two sentences in the box below, and see how many fuzzy words and phrases you could clarify or challenge using the techniques that we've covered in this chapter. These two sentences are quoted in the Australian Prudential Regulatory Authority (APRA) Report into Irregular Currency Options Trading at the National Australia Bank in March 2004 and are from an internal National Australia Bank Market Risk report delivered to the bank's Commercial and Institutional Banking Risk Management Executive Committee in November 2003, several months prior to the bank's forex trading losses of $360 million being made public.

Exercise:

Write the questions (including the fuzzy words) in the space provided below.

"At the time of writing, (Global Markets Division) trading operations continue to manage risk responsibly in changing market conditions. Adherence to risk discipline is good."

When you've done that, place a tick next to the two or three questions that you feel will provide the best data for ensuring that the company's interests are looked after.

The language in those two sentences is typical 'corporate speak'. It is easy to accept the language at face value on your first reading of those sentences, or when that language is used in discussions during meetings. However, the language is at the high end of the 'fuzzy' spectrum, and is fairly meaningless.

If you understand the language patterns that the **Powerful Questions** are designed to challenge, you'll hear warning bells ringing in those two sentences, even if you don't know anything about currency trading or the NAB's processes.

The warning bells do not necessarily mean that something *is* wrong. They are a means of raising awareness that something *may* be wrong, and that it might be wise to ask further questions.

The NAB's losses were associated with what has been called rogue trading, where the trades are made outside the bank's guidelines, in this case over a period of time.

In the following table I have taken each word or phrase and indicated:

- the possible effect of the word/phrase on the listener's awareness

- questions that might be asked

- some follow up questions that could be anticipated from the context of the quote, even if you know nothing about forex trading.

Words/phrases	Awareness	Possible questions
At the time of writing	This phrase diverts attention from other time frames and limits remaining text to the nominated time frame. It contracts, directs and focuses awareness to a specific time. However, the actual time frame is not specified. The document may have been dated, but written some time earlier.	What do you mean by 'At the time of writing'? When specifically? What was the position prior to the report being written? What is the position since?
trading operations	Global phrase which induces expanded awareness, fuzzy direction and fuzzy focus. If there is a variety of trading operations, this phrase obscures which trading activity is referred to. The total activities may average out to be 'responsible' or 'good', but the risk exposure on any one type of trading activity could be unacceptable.	What specifically do you mean by trading operations? Which trading operations specifically are you referring to?
continue	Global, unspecified period – from when? Expands awareness over an undefined period. Suggests long term whereas the opening phrase related to a specific time.	What do you mean by 'continue'? Since when/what time frame? What specifically was the risk profile prior to the current report period? What would I see if you showed me the risk profiles over that period?

Words/phrases	Awareness	Possible questions
to manage	Global term, expands awareness, could mean different things in the context.	What specifically do you mean by 'manage'? What are your target risk outcomes? What are your actual risk outcomes?
risk	Global term, nature of risk is not specified. This word may encompass many risks, averaged to be managed 'responsibly'.	What risks specifically? What is the current exposure? Show me the figures. How, specifically, are you managing risk?
responsibly	Global term, no measure specified. Expands awareness. Interpretation of circumstances, not factual.	What do you mean by responsibly? Based on what criteria? What do you see/ hear that tells you that risk is being managed responsibly?
in changing market conditions	Global language, unspecified market, unspecified conditions. Nature and extent of change is unspecified. Expands awareness.	Which market conditions are changing? How specifically are they changing? What specifically are you doing to manage those changing conditions responsibly?

Words/phrases	Awareness	Possible questions
Adherence	Global term. Noun used where in fact the act of adhering is a verb. Unspecified person taking that action.	What do you mean by 'adherence?' Who specifically is adhering to risk disciplines? What specifically are they doing to adhere to risk disciplines?
to risk discipline	Global term. Nature of risk is not specified. The 'discipline' is unspecified	Which risks specifically are you referring to? Which risk disciplines are you referring to? Which of those are being adhered to fully? Which are not being adhered to fully? What is our current exposure? Show me the figures. How does that compare to the required risk discipline?
is good	Interpretation of unspecified facts.	What specifically do you mean by 'good'? Where is 'good' on a scale of 1 – 10 where 1 is disregard of risk discipline and 10 is full compliance? Where is compliance not good?

Since the language in the quoted sentences is on the high fuzzy end of the spectrum, the questions in the right hand column are designed to contract, direct and focus awareness by seeking specifics. Questions that seek specific data are the antidote to fuzzy language.

The words that, when challenged, are most likely to gain useful information for decisions are 'manage risk responsibly' and 'adherence to risk discipline is good'.

A little further down the page of the APRA report are some more interesting 'bell-ringing' quotes. APRA conducted an on-site review with NAB in August 2003, and an **Questions that seek specific data are the antidote to fuzzy language.** annual prudential consultation in December 2003, just a couple of months before the bank's trading losses of $360 million became public. APRA states in its report that during those meetings it (APRA) was explicitly informed that *'average FX and volatility (option) exposures were relatively static'* and that NAB's trading profile was *'conservative'* (italics added).

The words quoted in italics are in the 'high fuzzy' range and are not particularly meaningful ('average', ' exposures', 'relatively', 'conservative'). The APRA report went on to say that those statements 'were not a reasonable representation of the true picture and were patently misleading'.

Where compliance, investigations, verification or due diligence are required (see Chapter 4), it is useful to look behind the fuzzy language, interpretations, opinions and assumptions by asking to see the hard evidence on which the claims are based.

Review

✓ When what was said may be important, ask for the conversation to be described in quotes

✓ Leaders must have the confidence and competence to stay 'present' with the real issues, and to ask questions that probe, elicit, clarify and verify the facts, assumptions, processes and meaning contained in written documents and in conversations.

✓ Which 20% of fuzzy language will, when clarified, give you 80% of the meaning that will lead to a result?

✓ *Time:* When, specifically. *Space:* Where, specifically? *Measure:* How much, specifically?

✓ You always have the ability to clarify what you mean and what other people mean.

✓ Specific = sensory data. Sensory data is what you see, hear, feel, smell and taste.

Cascading to Level 3 sensory data (see, hear, feel) is the key to clarifying meaning and facts:

> *What do you mean by...?*

> *What specifically do you mean by...?*

> *What did/do/would you see/hear/feel...?*

✓ As a rule of thumb, focus on '*What...?*', then '*How?*'

✓ Make '*How can we improve it?*' a standard question.

Practice suggestions

The following suggestions will help you develop greater awareness of the fuzzy language patterns. Practice at your own pace. You will find it useful to spread the following items over a few days, taking one or two components of the questions at a time, and practising them as often as possible in a day. The listening components can be passive e.g. listening to others speak on a train or bus, or at a café.

1 Take a few minutes to complete the exercises in this chapter if you haven't already done so. (Other exercises are available at www.powerfulquestions.net and www.spandah.com)

2 Over the next few days:

- Review a recent report, proposal, briefing paper or strategic document. Identify the fuzzy language and use the questions in this section to challenge or clarify the language. If you find any words or phrases that you'd like to clarify, call the person who presented the document and ask the questions, if appropriate.

- Review the documents for your next meeting and highlight the fuzzy words and phrases. Consider which of the marked items will be of most value to clarify, and formulate the questions you will ask initially, with follow up questions. In larger meetings, you'll need to get to the point quickly, as others will cut in with their own questions. One-on-one discussions provide a good vehicle to practise asking cascade questions and probing deeper.

- Practise listening to news services, talk-back radio, interviews and conversations specifically for the purpose of identifying fuzzy nouns, fuzzy verbs, the 'not' word, interpretations etc, and coining the questions you'd ask.

- Practise listening to lengthy discussions, keeping track of the most important word/phrase to challenge at the end of a sentence or paragraph, and asking the questions.

- Ask the questions in a conversational manner to maintain rapport.

3

Identifying a Process, Strategy or Model

Chapter 3

IDENTIFYING A PROCESS, STRATEGY OR MODEL

There's an old song that goes something like this: _"It ain't what you do it's the way that you do it; that's what gets results."_

My father tried to teach me that lesson many years ago. I wish I'd listened more carefully at the time. It refers to probably the most important process in business. If I were permitted to teach only one of the **Powerful Questions**, this would be it.

Eliciting a process

The skill of eliciting a process through asking questions can be very useful for modeling past, present and future actions, decisions and strategies. It enables you to understand

- how something was done
- how things are being done
- how something will be done

and how each can be improved.

The same questions can be used to understand the strategies, behaviours, choices, decisions, attitudes and thinking processes that created

- a successful outcome,
- an unsuccessful outcome.

Other people can then be coached, trained or mentored to repeat that success, or to improve performance.

We usually have more opportunities to learn from what _didn't_ work than from what *did* work. Few people are blessed with the ability to get everything right first time, especially when doing something new or different, as every company

We usually have more opportunities to learn from what *didn't* work than from what *did* work.

must do if it is to adapt, compete and grow successfully. That is why a culture which punishes mistakes and calculated risks, instead of learning from them and correcting them, will be driven by fear and blame and will not be competitive or responsive. Fear stifles innovation and initiative.

Directors, executives and managers can play a pivotal role in creating a learning culture.

FUZZY VERBS (again)

You'll recall the following example that we considered earlier, in the section *Fuzzy Language Techniques.*

Example: *"I'd suggest we let the audit committee handle this."*

In this example, the word 'handle' is unclear in two respects – what the word *means* and to what *process* the word refers.

We looked at how to clarify the meaning of the verb 'handle' by asking the question *"What specifically do you mean by 'handle'?"*

In this example, the speaker may mean fix, investigate, get rid of, cover up, etc. Now we'll look at how to clarify the *process* of 'handle'.

Example: *'How, specifically, do we want them to handle/fix/*

Technique:

Clarifying Verb (Process)

*To identify the **process** ask: "How, specifically...?"*

---

investigate it?'

Asking the question *'How, specifically...'* not only identifies the process by which something is done, but also provides the information that enables you to assess how well the process works

and to challenge assumptions about what will work.
For instance:

> *"The business case developed for the project identified the potential to realise considerable cost savings."*

The obvious question is to ask 'What is the potential for cost savings?' or 'How much will we save?', but the most important issue is 'How are you going to save the costs?'. The person making that statement must have considered that a strategy was feasible for saving costs. But if the strategy is flawed, the costs savings will not be achieved. There are probably a number of assumptions underlying the statement, exemplified in the word 'potential' and 'considerable'. If we choose to clarify the verb, and ask:

> *'How, specifically, will you realise the cost savings?'*

the focus is shifted from the quantum of cost savings to the way that the cost savings will be achieved. The answer will probably be in the form of a broad strategy, because the language 'potential to realise considerable' is at the high end of the global/fuzzy spectrum and usually indicates that the details have not been thought through.

Let's say that the answer was:

> *"We'll cut staff in that area by 10% and save around $500,000 a year."*

The next question can then target possible shortcomings of the strategy:

> *"What impact will that have on the ability of the back room staff to monitor compliance with investment risk parameters?"*

A number of financial institutions have found that cutting back room staff can cause bigger losses than the predicted savings. In fact, many 'downsizing' cost cutting exercises have boosted short term financials but decimated longer term performance. We'll look at how to uncover unwanted 'flow-on' effects in Chapter 6 - *(The Ripple Effect: Identifying Hidden Purpose and Implications.)*

If you wanted to test the quality of the strategy for saving costs you might choose to cascade down on the process by which staff will be cut:

Q: *How, specifically will you cut staff?*

A: *We'd look to do it by natural attrition combined with good redundancy packages.*

Q: *How would you structure the redundancy packages?*

The answer will again give some clues as to whether the strategy will work, or how it can be improved. Generally improvements require a simple form of question:

How can we ...[state outcome and conditions]?

e.g.

How can we save costs without adversely impacting our ability to function?

or

How can we do this differently and still achieve the outcome but without the downside of the current strategy?

Modelling and improvement

I use the term modelling here to mean identifying and improving the process by which something was or will be done, so that the process can be transferred to others by way of coaching, mentoring or training.

Modelling not only involves identifying behaviours and action steps, but can also entail identifying 'mind processes' such as attitudes, thought processes, decision-making processes, analytical and judgment processes. Generally, the mind pro-cesses have more impact on success and failure than do actions. Actions are external events that are guided by the internal mind processes, which in turn are shaped by the processes of consciousness mentioned earlier. The external actions are objectively perceived by the senses of any observer, and are executed relatively slowly by physical means. The internal processes, on the other hand, are extraordinarily powerful, quick, complex and subtle – so much so that we generally do not notice them. We are usually only aware of the outcome of those processes – e.g. the idea or the decision. However, if we can identify the specific internal processes that create a successful outcome, and build them into a model that can be replicated by others, the 'soft' factors that make a difference to performance are no longer a struggle or a mystery.

In our live workshops we demonstrate how to model the subtle processes of consciousness in an exercise that uses a visual image which can be seen a number of different ways. Most people will initially see the image in one particular way. By changing their perception process, they will see a different image, even though nothing has changed on the screen. The change has not happened on the screen, but in the consciousness of the observer. When asked '*How did you change the image*' the participants invariably say "*I just changed it*" or "*I blinked*". However, after a few minutes of observing their own mind operate they begin to understand, and get a feel for, the series of internal processes that occur almost instantaneously by which the external world seems to change before their eyes. Their awareness moves beyond the mere outcome – a changed image – to noticing the processes of consciousness that shape and re-shape their reality. Once they are aware of the internal processes by which they create the change, they can replicate it at will, without effort. Those same processes are the substratum of change in organisations. Most change initiatives fail to live up to expectations, take longer to bed down, or cost more than anticipated because they are imposed by changing the external environment without first changing the 'internal' environment and the change is resisted, not fully embraced, and not owned by the people affected by the change.

That shift to 'observer' can be achieved by the application of the 'how' question, phrased so as to direct the mind to observe itself.

When we are able to observe that flow of consciousness we are in the genius state, from where it is easier to create the reality that we want. It is also a place from which intuitive understanding of our communication with others arises.

When we are able to observe that flow of consciousness we are in the genius state.

A good example of the practical application of those principles occurred a couple of years ago when I made a presentation to a large UK government organisation. The organisation was looking for a coaching model that could be applied to its executives, and our **Coach MasterProcess** was one of the short-listed processes. I was asked at the interview to demonstrate the process. One of the panel of interviewers volunteered to be the guinea pig. Her issue was that she'd applied three times for promotions in the past, and each time had not been appointed to the positions. She had again applied for another, more senior position and the interview was scheduled for the next week. I asked her to outline the way that she had previously approached the job interviews, and to pinpoint the points of failure. She identified one particular issue that seemed to be her weakness – she 'choked' whenever she was asked a difficult question that she had not anticipated. She was even anticipating that she would choke at the next interview. This is an ideal scenario for working on mastering the internal processes that create our reality.

I only asked her questions – mainly 'how' questions. The questions were phrased to enable her to draw on her own experience and on that deeper part of herself that knows what she needs. She considered previous instances in which she had successfully managed her internal state when taken by surprise

The questions were phrased to enable her to draw on her own experience and on that deeper part of herself that knows what she needs.

and challenged, and how to break that experience into components that could then be modelled and transferred to an interview. She considered a variety of ways to handle the prospective interview, and in particular how to deal with the unexpected, difficult and challenging questions. We did not consider the nature or content of potential questions that she might be asked, but instead identified the state of awareness that would give her the power to adapt effortlessly to any question and provide a response that flowed easily without stress. She then created a model that would work for her, tested it with her colleagues on the panel, and in the physical environment (actual room) where the interview would take place and made adjustments until she was fully congruent with the process. Her physical appearance was transformed during this exercise, and she radiated a serene confidence. The whole exercise took only about 45 minutes. She won the promotion a week later and that organisation became our client.

In the debriefing immediately after that exercise I asked the subject about her internal experience during the exercise. She started to say *"When you told me to do..."*, at which point a panel member interrupted and said *"He didn't tell you to do anything. I was listening, and he only asked you questions. You figured it all out yourself."*

We have the answers within us to the important questions about ourselves and our performance. All we need is the right process to bring the answers to the surface. That process is the *'How?'* question.

Those readers who may be interested in delving more into that topic and its application to empowerment, leadership and change in organisations will find more in my books ***Awakening the Spirit of the Corporation*** available at *www.spandah.com*

Technique:

4-Step Modelling and Improvement Process

1 Obtain an overview of the strategy, identifying the key steps and events in a sequential order, with general clarification, not a lot of detail

2 Listen for the critical points that caused the success or failure or, for future actions, the critical points that may cause success or failure. Ask

   "What are the critical points at which this succeeded/ failed?"

or,

   "What are the critical points at which this might succeed/fail?"

3 Drill down into the specific process and components of each step *("How specifically did you/will you do it...?")*, cascading to sensory-specific detail for the points of success or failure *"What did you say/what did they say?"* , *"How did you say that? What tone of voice?"* etc.

4 Change the process, e.g: *"How can we do this differently so that it works (better) next time?"*

or

   Improve the process, e.g: *"How can we improve the process so that we get better results?"*

That technique (in fact, all of the **Powerful Questions**) can be readily applied to

- strategic planning sessions

- change management

- process improvements

- quality control

- Six Sigma applications

- product development

- performance management

- contract and project management

- coaching

- meetings

- negotiations

and in a myriad of other business situations.

The third and fourth steps in the *4-Step Modelling and Improvement Process* are where you pay most attention. If a component of the strategy is critical, drive deeper into the sensory data until the actions taken or required to be taken are crystal clear.

It may be more appropriate to deal with that part of the process outside of a formal meeting, as it can often involve coaching to an extent that does not fit into a group.

Example: Resistance to change

An example is managing resistance to change. Let's say that the company wants to instal a new IT system, and the overview (Step 1) identifies staff *'buy-in'* as a major component of the strategy. The new system will enable the company to reduce staff numbers in administrative areas, and will also require all remaining staff to be trained in the newer, whiz-bang system.

> Q: *What are the critical points at which this might succeed or fail?*

A: The major area of risk is the staff response. The changeover to the new system is time-sensitive and we cannot afford to have resistance to the change from the folks who'll be operating the system.

The critical issue is the changeover. If it is time-sensitive, clarify the details:

Q: When is the changeover scheduled?

A: Two months from next weekend.

Q: What do you mean by time-sensitive?

A: The switch to the new system must occur over a weekend. We can't run both systems in parallel because they are not compatible. We can manage with fifty errors a day on start-up, by making corrections manually, but if the error rate exceeds that, then we will quickly find a backlog created that will adversely impact on most of our operations. In the past, we've found that when staff resist or don't like the changes, error rates are much higher than that.

This is an ideal opportunity to identify learnings from the past, so that they can be modelled into the present situation:

Q: How did you introduce the changes to staff on those past occasions?

A: We sent around a memo telling them what was happening, and provided the extra training that they needed.

Q: Did that work?

A: Not very well. The transition was slow and, as I said, there were many errors. It took several months before the staff were reasonably happy with the changes. The time-critical element was not an issue on those occasions, so we were lucky, because there were a number of hiccups with the system and implementation that had to be fixed after the system went live.

'Hiccups' is a super-fuzzy term. If we clarify what happened, and how the hiccups were remedied, that will probably provide some of the model for the current situation, or for another future situation. Even if the hiccups are different to the present issues, the way that they were dealt with may be transferable to the present situation. The main thing is to go with the flow of what is being said, as long as it remains on track. That way the continuity of the questions will be seamless. It requires that you really listen and stay present with the discussion, keeping the structure of the four-step technique in mind but at the same time exploring the issues that are raised by the language.

Q: *What were the hiccups?*

A: *Mainly that the software system did not interface very neatly with the established work practices, and there were also some environmental issues and safety issues.*

There are three items mentioned in that answer – interface, environmental and safety issues. Make a mental note of those three items and allow the conversation to flow around them. The environmental and safety issues were mentioned together, and were the last items mentioned, so the discussion will probably flow on quite smoothly by picking up on those words. They are often inter-related and it is safe to allow the person to choose whether to deal with them as a package or separately. You can always refer specifically to one or the other if necessary.

Q: *Such as?*

A: *The computer monitors were a bit larger than the previous monitors, and took up more desk space. That placed the screens closer to the operator and there was some concern about increased radiation and glare..*

This is probably a planning error.

> *Q:* *How did you plan the environmental and safety issues on those occasions?*

> *A:* *We didn't check dimensions of the monitors or match them to the desk sizes. In fact, we made a lot of assumptions and mainly focused on the software and hardware together with the outcomes we expected, rather than how the whole process would work for the staff.*

This admission implies that one of the learnings was to plan for the impact of the change on staff. You can press further for specifics, but that can be brought out later if necessary. The next question refers back to the interface matter, before it is forgotten and while it is still in context:

> *Q:* *And what were the interface issues?*

> *A:* *The forms that we had been using had data entry fields in different positions to the previous forms and did not match the sequence of activities carried out by the operators. The activities were in the correct order, so we had to redesign the forms.*

Another error in pre-planning. This is likely to be part of the current solution (or problem if not dealt with) since there is a repeat pattern in behaviour. The project planning process may need to be changed. The questioner will coax the questions in that direction if the person answering doesn't realise what the failure pattern has been.

> *Q:* *How did you plan the interface issues?*

> *A:* *We told the software provider what our procedures were and they wrote the program accordingly. However, it was not until the system was operating that we realised there were problems with sequences of data fields.*

Here is a clue to a better planning model. The answer omits stating who discovered the problems, but implies that operators probably had something to do with it.

Q: *How was that discovered?*

A: *The staff actually pointed that out and made some suggestions that were adopted.*

The next question will highlight the learning by directing the person's awareness to one of the lessons from the past experience:

Q: *Would it have been useful to have that input from staff prior to implementation?*

A: *Yes, definitely.*

Notice how the questions move effortlessly around the discussion, identifying the issues and solutions, so that a workable model can be elicited. Now we'll move forward to the present circumstances and transfer the learnings. First, obtain more clarity around what outcome is wanted. The next question will withdraw awareness from the past, redirect it to the near future and emanate (create) the desired reality in awareness. There is also an element of vision required in the answer, which means that the person's awareness will expand. There should be a feeling of relief and upliftment with the answer.

Q: *So, what outcome do you want with the current project?*

A: *A smooth transition, on time, with zero errors and with full staff support.*

Q: *How do you propose to generate staff support and buy-in?*

The question is framed to include 'buy-in', which accommodates participation, not simply passive support. The phrase 'staff support' is also included, to ensure that the person answering is not negated.

A: *We'll hold staff presentations and explain the reasons*

*why the new system is needed and what it will entail
from their viewpoint.*

This answer does not specifically reflect the earlier learning about staff involvement prior to implementation. It appears to describe a passive event. The next question clarifies that point.

Q: *What format would the presentation take?*

A: *A PowerPoint presentation followed by questions and answers.*

A talk-fest. The next question directs awareness to the 'buy-in' issue.

Q: *On a scale of of 1 to 10, where 10 is maximum buy-in, what level of buy-in do you believe that process will achieve, based on your past experience?*

A: *Well, I'm hoping for full commitment.*

That did not answer the question, and avoided commitment.

Q: *Sure, but what do you realistically expect from that strategy?*

A: *[Pause] Maybe a six or seven.*

'*Maybe*' is not a strong commitment. The strategy will fail if the designer has little enthusiasm. The strategy needs a major injection of fresh ideas.

Q: *Is that good enough for what you need?*

A: *[Pause] I guess not. We really need more than that. We need a nine or a ten.*

The next question is framed to move more towards a high level of active participation of staff:

Q: *So how could you improve the strategy to gain commitment and ownership of nine plus?*

A: *Well, I suppose the staff would have to be more*

involved in design and implementation.

'Suppose' is a lazy statement, a 'fudge'.

Q: You suppose, or they would have to be?

A: No, they would have to be.

Q: And how could you design the process so that they were more involved, bearing in mind the things you learned from the previous change initiatives?

That question directed the mind to the past learnings and transferred them to the current situation.

A: Well, we have two months before being operational so we could get the staff to look at potential problems and solutions before we have to 'go live'.

Now is the time to raise the bar, improve the strategy and begin to create actions that give substance to the ownership and commitment of staff.

Q: How would you do that so that you get the maximum buy-in, commitment and on-time implementation?

A: Ask staff for help in designing the implementation, identifying problems and developing solutions. Instead of telling them what is needed, we could conduct the session as a workshop in which they work in groups to consider the problems that might be encountered, and improvements that might work better than what we have in mind. They could also design the environmental and health and safety solutions. You never know, they might even come up with some software design solutions that will work better in our applications.

Q: How would you ask them for help – what would you say?

A: *I'd tell them that we need their assistance to make the changes work...*

Q: *Put it in quotes for me, as best you can. What would you actually say?*

Always have the critical conversations practised in quotes:

A: *Mmm. I'd say "We've learned from previous change initiatives that management doesn't always get implementation right – as you probably know - and that the folks who are impacted by the change are far more qualified to design the details of implementation and integration of the new system. The last time we tried something like this we didn't get your input until after the 'go live' date. This time, we'd like to have your help well before the implementation date, so that there is less stress and the system works in a practical way that is easy for you to use. What I'm inviting you to do is to spend the morning working through the various issues and potential problems that this system might raise, not only in functionality, but also the environmental and health and safety issues that may be of concern to you, and any other issues that we may not have considered."*

Q: *How does that feel on a scale of 1 – 10?*

A: *Pretty good, actually.*

Always test to see if there is a way to improve.

Q: *Could you improve it?*

A: *Yes, I'm sure that I can, but I think I'll spend a little time putting together the whole package, including preliminary material that the attendees will receive prior to the workshop, so we can set the scene.*

The next question tests whether the new strategy is more congruent with the desired outcome:

Q: And if you took that approach, how would you rate the likelihood of staff buy-in, commitment and ownership?

A: With a bit more thought, I think we can get to at least nine, maybe ten.

Give direction, feedback and arrange a follow-up session to ensure that the plan is completed:

Q: Good. The approach you've just described is a much better strategy in my opinion. Could you let me have the detailed workshop agenda and process in, say, two days' time?

A: It's a bit tight, as I'll be interstate all day tomorrow. Three days would be OK.

Q: That's fine with me.

The person answering the questions now '*owns*' the revised strategy, which is far more likely to succeed.

In that example, the questioner dealt with both what didn't work on previous occasions (and how to improve it) and how to improve a future strategy. Both can be captured and developed into a model for future use in similar situations, as part of organisational learning.

Softener

If you believe you may encounter some resistance to Step 1, use a softener such as:

'I'm not quite clear here on how this was/will be implemented. Can you just give me an overview of the steps that were/will be undertaken?'

Learning and growth

The 'How' process can be applied to improving the performance of your team, and your own performance.

Many companies operate in a culture of fear, where personal responsibility is avoided and blame is passed to others. When that culture is ingrained at Board or executive level, there is little hope for the rest of the organization.

Moving out of an unhealthy culture of blame, excuses self-justification, avoidance of responsibility and negative action or inaction, and into a healthy culture of honesty, integrity, responsibility, accountability and positive action requires answers to sometimes tough questions about what didn't work.

One of the most effective, and fastest way to grow as humans and as companies is to

- recognise and accept when something is not working

- accept responsibility for it not working

- understand the process by which it did not work

- learn what not to do next time

- learn what to do next time

- develop a workable process

- put in place the culture and processes that enable success on the next occasion.

The other side of the organisational learning coin is to look at the successes - identify what worked, and to model and replicate that, i.e. elicit the processes (external and internal) that generated the successful result or outcome and embed that model in the organization.

Whether we are learning from something that didn't work, or something that did work, we must identify:

➢ what did/didn't work

➢ what to do instead, and how to do it so that it does work/ how to improve the process further

> ➤ how to embed the success model in the company's culture, style and behaviours.

The 'how' question is a powerful tool – probably the single most useful tool - for doing that.

Note that the first point does not say 'what went wrong'. The word 'wrong' goes hand in hand with 'right'. They are not particularly useful words because they are usually based on opinion, create a mutually exclusive dichotomy, and have overtones of blame, which creates resistance.

It is generally more useful to focus on

> ➤ what works

> ➤ what doesn't work, and

> ➤ what can be done to make it work better, how to improve things.

That does not prevent particular persons being identified as the cause of an event, if indeed that is the case, but it does enable the focus to be directed towards events, behaviours, attitudes and skills, which can then be corrected. This approach enables ego to be kept to a minimum, and reduces the need for a scapegoat and consequent loss of talent.

A strong culture of self-assessment and learning is a bonus for investors. Any Director, executive or manager who thinks that he/she has nothing more to learn is foolish. The world is changing far too fast for that attitude to survive.

The following questions will assist your team to improve, and learn from mistakes. Select a decision that you consider to have been a poor team decision, and fill in the blank sections under each question. There's no value to you in just reading the questions. The value is in answering the questions. Every leader has made decisions that did not work for some reason. Smart business leaders will take the time to consider how their decision-making process can be improved.

Technique:
The Team's Role

1. What did we do as a Board/executive/management team that might have enabled or allowed this to occur?

2. What did we *not* do as a Board/executive/ management team that might have enabled or allowed this to occur?

3. What do we as a Board/executive/management team need to do (differently) to ensure that it does not recur?

4. How do we embed this as part of our Board/executive/ management team learning?

If a decision failed, the examination must go beyond the decision making 'system', and the tenet 'Know thyself' applied. Self-reflection can be done in the privacy of your own mind. If you are serious about growth and improvement, self-reflection is essential. It takes courage and requires self-honesty. If you take the attitude that you can improve what you are doing to the benefit of yourself, your family, your business, your stakeholders and community, then honest self-reflection will not be difficult, and will prove to be a powerful example for your staff to follow.

Select a decision you made which you feel might have been done better by you, in hindsight, then answer the following questions:

Exercise:

Use the technique for clarifying the verb's process in the following reports using the *"How, specifically...?'* form of question:

Technique:
Self-reflection

1 *How did I handle this when it came before me/the Board/executive/management team?*

2 *What choices did I have available?*

3 *What choices did I make?*

4 *In hindsight, what could I have done differently to improve my decision-making ability and my interactions on the Board/executive/management team?*

5 *How will I handle a similar situation in future ?*

---

1 *Executives propose to meet with the other parties in the near future to discuss the implications of the fallout between the major partners to the project and the unions. The primary focus will be clarifying the issues between them that have caused the problems that we are now facing, and how to progress the project so that it works for all parties.*

2 *At the time of writing, [Global Markets Division] trading operations continue to manage risk responsibly in changing market conditions. Adherence to risk discipline is good.*

Review

- ✓ You can ask questions to understand how something was done, how things are being done and how something will be done, plus how each can be improved.

- ✓ The same questions can be used to model a successful outcome, or an unsuccessful outcome.

- ✓ Other people can then be coached, trained or mentored to repeat that success, or to improve performance.

- ✓ We usually have more opportunities to learn from what *didn't* work than from what did work.

- ✓ To identify the process ask: *"How, specifically...?"*

- ✓ Asking the question *'How, specifically...'* not only identifies the process by which something is done, but also provides the information that enables you to assess how well the process works and to challenge assumptions about what will work.

- ✓ We have the answers within us to the important questions about ourselves and our performance. All we need is the right process to bring the answers to the surface.

- ✓ *4-Step Modelling and Improvement Process*: Obtain an overview of the key steps of the strategy; listen for the critical points that caused or may cause the success or failure; drill down into the specific process and components of each step, cascading to sensory-specific detail for the points of success or failure; change or improve the process.

✓ The 'How' process can be applied to improving the performance of your team, and your own performance.

✓ Identify what did/didn't work, what to do instead, how to do it so that it does work/how to improve the process further, and how to embed the success model in the company's culture, style and behaviours.

✓ A strong culture of self-assessment and learning is a bonus for investors. Any Director, executive or manager who thinks that he/she has nothing more to learn is foolish. The world is changing far too fast for that attitude to survive.

✓ Self-reflection can be done in the privacy of your own mind. If you are serious about growth and improvement, self-reflection is essential. It takes courage and requires self-honesty.

✓ Remember - you can use the 3-step sensory cascade with verbs
   - How would you do that?
   - How, specifically?
   - What would you see/hear if you did it successfully?

✓ If in doubt about whether to clarify meaning or process, ask
   - What do you mean by (verb) first, followed by
   - How did you/would you do it?

Practice suggestions

1   Take a few minutes to complete the exercises in this section, if you have not already done so.

2   Over the next few days:

- Practise listening to news services, talk-back radio, interviews and conversations specifically for the purpose of identifying verbs that do not specify the process described by the verb, and ask aloud *'How did/would you do that?'*, *'How specifically did/would you do that?'* and *'What would I see you do, hear you say, feel happening if I was present while you did that?'*

- Practise listening to lengthy discussions, keeping track of the verbs that do not sufficiently specify the process described by the verb, and ask the *'How...?'* question.

- Review a recent report, proposal, briefing paper or strategic document. Identify the verbs and use the 'How' question that would elicit the process. If you find any words or phrases that you'd like to clarify, call the person who presented the document and ask them the question, if appropriate.

-   Review the documents for your next meeting and highlight the verbs. Consider which of the highlighted items will be of most value to clarify and formulate the questions you will ask initially, and any follow-up questions.

- Ask the questions in a conversational manner to maintain rapport

4

Challenging Facts, Opinions,

Beliefs and Assumptions,

and Verifying 'Facts'.

CHALLENGING FACTS, OPINIONS, BELIEFS AND ASSUMPTIONS AND VERIFYING FACTS

M y friends and I thought that Mr Barnett was the best teacher at school. Mr Barnett was our high school history teacher. He told jokes in every lesson, for most of the lesson. One day he became serious and said :

> *"At the next lesson I'm going to introduce you to the most important lesson in the study of history. For that purpose I want you to read Chapter 4 in the European history text. In that chapter there is a reference to Count Metternich and in particular his meeting with the leader of another country. I'll ask you questions about that meeting."*

We thought this must be serious stuff if old Barnett was foregoing his favourite past time to actually teach us something.

At the next lesson Mr Barnett asked if we'd read the chapter on Metternich. We had. Then he asked us a question about the particular meeting between Metternich and a head of state. We dutifully answered the question.

Then Mr Barnett asked: *"How do you know that?"*. We were a bit puzzled by the question, but basically, we said *"That's what's in the text"*.

"Here is your history lesson", said Mr Barnett.

"When I was a PhD student at university, I wrote a thesis on Metternich. There was not much material available in the library on that particular event, so I travelled to Europe and spend two wonderful months fossicking through the great European libraries and having a good time. When I returned home, I finished my thesis and was granted my doctorate. That particular event that you read about in the text is, in fact from my doctoral thesis. You'll find it in many texts now, though they rarely cite my thesis as the source. I don't mind, because it isn't true. I couldn't find any source material about that meeting between Metternich and the head of state, so I made it up, and concocted a source reference. It's now part of history. Don't believe everything you read. Most of the 'facts' that you 'know' are not facts. They are someone's opinion, belief or interpretation. Sometimes they are pure imagination, but others assume that they are verifiable and repeat the 'fact' until it becomes part of reality."

Mr Barnett was a history crook, but he understood an important fact about perception and reality.

He was right. Statements of 'fact' are often actually statements of opinion or belief, or are assumptions or interpretations, and are the cause of many poor decisions and failed strategies. They create a reality that, if accepted, limits the listener's decision-making ability.

In this chapter we'll look at six techniques:

- Clarifying the source
- Challenging the interpretation
- Absolutes
- Universals
- Fudging
- 'Feeling' statements.

Clarifying the source

This technique is very effective for dealing with assumptions. A couple of years ago, a UK businessman flew to Australia to attend one of my programs. He was jet lagged for the first day of the two-day workshop, and was nodding off to sleep from time to time. However, when we reached this technique he became fully awake and very excited. He said to me later *"If I'd known that technique ten years ago, I'd have saved myself millions of pounds."*

The key to this technique is to challenge the other person to produce source evidence in the form of sensory data – what was seen, heard, felt, smelled and tasted.

The third point is very important. If you are making a decision based

---

Technique:
Verifying facts, challenging assumptions, opinions and interpretations

1 *How do you know that (to be true/accurate)?*

2 *What did you see/hear/feel* that leads to that conclusion/what are the facts and circumstances on which you base that?*

3 *What's the evidence?*

  - *How do we know that [the evidence] is correct?*

  - *Show me the [evidence].*

  - *How was [the evidence] obtained?*

* Deal with one sense at a time.

---

on critical data, and a lot is at stake, get the source information if possible, and verify the source.

The last question in that technique - *"How was [the evidence] obtained?"* - is often overlooked. It refers to the quality of the evidence. Fans of the popular TV show CSI (Crime Scene Investigators) will be familiar with the questions that are asked about contaminated evidence. The way that evidence is collected, stored or handle may influence the results of forensic examination. In 2005, Bradley Murdoch was convicted in Darwin, Australia for the alleged murder of an English tourist, Peter Falconio, on a remote outback road in central Australia. The home-made handcuffs used to bind Falconio's girlfriend, Joanne Lees, contained DNA alleged to belong to Murdoch. Lees escaped her assailant and hid in the bush beside the road. The handcuffs were retrieved from Lees after she was rescued by a passing truck driver, and were stored on a shelf in a police evidence room with Murdoch's personal items that were obtained from Murdoch some months after the alleged murder. The DNA in the handcuffs is the evidence, but the way that the items were stored and handled was an issue at trial because of the risk that DNA from Murdoch's personal items may have been transferred to the handcuffs when stored or handled in police custody.

In the business context, an example of when the question *"How was [the evidence] obtained?"* would be appropriate is when a decision relies on a survey result. The survey may suggest a particular result, but the quality of the survey will depend on which questions were asked in the survey. A slight change in the questions will produce a different result. A change to the sampling technique may also alter the result.

A note on asking questions (Technique #2) related to the senses: Deal with each sense separately, starting with the most relevant sense for the data – e.g. for conversations:

> *What specifically did you hear?,*

or

> *What specifically did they say?.*

'My experience'

When people are asked *'How do you know it will work/won't work?'* or *'How do you know that's true?'* you will often hear the response 'My experience'. Whilst experience is valuable in many situations, it can also be offered as a means of manipulating a decision. 'Experience' is one of the fuzziest words you'll hear. It is simply a way of descibing, in one word, many events that occurred over a period of time and interpretations of those events.

It is perfectly legitimate to ask the person about their experience. You'll usually find fuzzy descriptions are given in response, together with assumptions, interpretations and beliefs that have been filtered extensively.

With statements of experience, ask for sensory data about the person's experience and for differences between the current circumstances and the circumstances of the person's past experience:

> *How was that done/how did you do it/what happened on those occasions?*

> *Specifically?*

> *What did you see/hear/feel?*

> *Were the circumstances different from the current circumstances? How?*

You are then in a better position to make an informed decision based on better factual information rather than on someone else's self-declared experience.

Challenging the interpretation/meaning

Where the sensory data has been identified clearly but could be interpreted another way, (for instance, a conversation given in quotes where it appears to you that the words could have a different meaning attributed to them than the way they were understood by the listener – e.g. in a dispute) ask the following:

Technique:
Challenging the interpretation / meaning

Is it possible that what you saw/heard/felt
[the evidence] could mean something other than X?
*   -If so, what else, other than X?*
*   - Anything else?*

Or:

If [another person] was observing/listening, do you
think it might be possible for them to understand that
another way?
*   -How else, specifically?*

Then:

How might those other ways affect the situation?

How do you know which understanding is correct?
*   -How can you find out?*
*   - How else?*

Absolutes

'Absolutes' are words that allow no exception to actions or process. They are usually used to limit behaviour and contract awareness, albeit unintentionally. They often reflect a difference in values and risk profile of the people communicating, and are commonly used to manipulate. Absolutes are words such as:

Can't	Have to	Should	Won't	Is	Certain
Must	Essential	Compulsory	No choice	Isn't	Must not

They generally reflect the opinion and values of the person using them, as opposed to stating a fact. People who are risk-averse or conservative by nature have an affinity for using Absolutes. People who want to exert authority to prevent certain behaviours or choices (such as parents with toddlers, or managers who want a decision to go a particular way) will use Absolutes to influence a decision or behaviour.

There are times, of course, when Absolutes correctly describe a situation, e.g. voting is compulsory in some countries, so the description 'compulsory' is a legal fact in those jurisdictions. However, that does not mean that you have no choice. You may choose not to vote, risk prosecution and choose to pay any fine that may be imposed if you are prosecuted.

There may be a condition attached to an Absolute that accurately defines the reality, such as

> *"We have to enter the accounts in this way if we are to comply with the legislation".*

However, it is also possible that that statement is not true. If you look at the legislation, it may not prescribe a particular way of entering accounts, but may define a standard that could be achieved in any of a number of ways.

Consider the following report:

> *Whilst elements of the business case should and must move forward (e.g. automation of customer transfers will be presented to ABC in June, ensuring operational cost reduction initiatives continue), the economic case for billing systems consolidation is now more complex and less obvious financially. To ensure that all of the latter and future projects that impact customer data are managed within clear context and framework, it is recommended that a joint business/IT customer data and information strategy be developed. To ensure balance, it is recommended this be facilitated by the projects office.*

The author of that report liked the word 'ensure', which means 'make certain'. That is another Absolute. The author twice states recommendations in the form *'To ensure that X occurs, it is recommended Y be done'*. That could be taken to mean 'Doing Y will ensure X outcome'. It could also imply that Y is the best, or even the only, way to ensure X.

That report encourages a number of specific decisions to be made. But can they be made on an informed basis on the information in that report? Perhaps. However, we can test the statements with some questions and perhaps gain some clarity around the recommendations and circumstances related in the report. Remember, the purpose of the **Powerful Questions** is not only to identify potential risks and flaws, and to correct them, but also to test the viability, veracity and accuracy of information, ideas and strategies on which we base decisions and investments. And, if possible, to improve strategies, processes and performance. We could test the claims by asking questions such as:

- *How can we be sure that Y will lead to X?*

- *How do we know that Y is the best way to achieve X?*

- *Is it possible that there may be a better way?*

- *The economic case for billing systems consolidation is less obvious financially? According to whom? Based on what evidence?*

- *Elements (which elements specifically?) should and must move forward? What would happen if they didn't? Is it possible that there is a better alternative? If there was a better alternative, what would it be?*

There are seven questioning patterns for challenging Absolutes:

Technique:
Challenging Absolutes

Ask yourself: Which of the following questions will provide the most useful shift of reality or thinking process [expand, contract, direct, focus, stillness]

1 *What would happen if... [we did/didn't] ?*

2 *How do you know...?*

3 *According to whom/Says who?*

4 *Is it possible that...? / Can you imagine...?*

5 *If...how...and/so that...?*

6 *You mean we don't know how to, yet?*

7 *Can't...yet?*

The following are examples of each technique (with some follow-on questions):

- It's vital that we take immediate action to proceed.
    *What would happen if we **did** take immediate action?*
    How do you know that would be the result?

and/or

    *What would happen if we **didn't** take immediate action?*
    How do you know that would be the result?

- It's mandatory that we meet the cost of time overruns.
    How do you know that it is mandatory?
    According to whom?
    Show me the contract terms.
    The terms are verbal? What, specifically, was said about payment of cost overruns?

- They won't agree to that course of action.
    According to whom?
    Says who?
    How do we know that?
    What specifically did they say or do that suggests that to be the case?

- We're stuck with this problem. It'll cost us dearly.
    Is it possible that there's another way around this problem that we haven't thought about yet?
    If so, what do you think it might be?

or

    Can you imagine that there may be another way out of this situation?

    If so, what do you think it might be?

- If we do it, we'll lose client A. If we don't do it, we'll lose client B. Each represents 20% of our revenue.

     *If we **did** do it, how could we do it so that we still retained client A?*

     *If we **didn't** do it, how could we manage the fallout and still retain client B?*

- It's impossible. It can't be done.

     We can't do it, yet?
     How could we develop the capability to do it?

or

     You mean we don't know how to do that, yet?
     How could we learn how to do it?

Each of these techniques can be used in combination when appropriate, e.g. taking the first, second and fifth techniques:

What would happen if we didn't take immediate action?

How do you know that would be the result?

If we didn't take immediate action, how could we manage the situation so that we avoid that risk?

Can't

The word 'can't' rates a special mention. It is commonly used in two ways, meaning:

- not allowed to... *"We can't give clients' names to third parties without permission."*

or

- not able to... *"We can't get the two sections of the product to match up."*

The first usage (permission) can be challenged with any of techniques 1 – 5, on page 174:

- We can't give clients' names to third parties without permission.

    What would happen if we did ?

    How do you know we can't ?

    According to whom/Says who?

    Is it possible that there may be a way we could legally give their names to third parties without permission ?

    If there was a way, how do you think we could do it without permission and not break the law?

Obviously you would choose whichever of those questions works best for the circumstances. You can also use those five techniques (particularly techniques 4 and 5) with the second usage (inability to do something), but technique 6 is very useful for first 'cracking the barrier', e.g.

- We can't get the two sections of the product to match up.

    You can't match them up, yet?

or

    You don't know how to match them up, yet?

The word 'yet' has the effect of limiting the perceived inability to the present. It means 'up until now', which implies that the future is open. In most cases where the word 'can't' is used to denote inablility, it actually denotes "*I don't know how to...*". You can then move quickly into solutions:

- We can't get the two sections of the product to match up.

    Q: You can't match them up, yet?

    A: That's right.

    Q: What do you think needs to be done to enable you to match them up?

    If you could match them up, how would you do it?

or

> Q: *You don't know how to match them up, yet?*
>
> A: *Correct.*
>
> Q: *Who do you think might be able to assist with solving this problem?*

There is also a shorter way of challenging 'can't'. This was created by Cyril Rouhliadeff, who was co-facilitating a workshop with me. We were always looking for better ways to obtain outcomes, and one day when we were demonstrating the *Challenging Absolutes* techniques to the workshop participants, Cyril thought of an even quicker way to challenge 'can't':

> *I can't.*
>
> Q: *...Yet?*

Do you recall the following example from the section on *Time, Space and Measure*, where the answer was found 100 years in the (imaginary) future?

> *"We've come up with a groundbreaking idea, but what we want to do is too advanced. We simply don't have the technology or science to do what would be required."*

In that example, the Absolute was 'don't', but the effect was 'we can't do it'. My first question was a single word:

> *....Yet?*

In other words, *'You don't have the technology or science, yet.'* From there it is easy to move into solutions because as soon as the person answers *'That's right'*, the doorway is open to finding a solution.

You'll find the sixth technique, or Cyril's technique, followed by technique five, to be very effective with young children when they become frustrated with trying to learn a new skill, such as riding a bike. They will sometimes say "I can't", with a screwed up face. If you leave it there, they'll convince themselves that they 'can't, forever', or so it will seem to them. Simply say 'Yet?' and you'll see the switch on their faces to a future possibility. Follow it by a learning or possibility question:

> *How do you think we might be able to learn this the easiest way?*

or

> *If you could do it, what would you do differently?*

and then guide them to learn.

Universals

Universals are words that allow no exception to issues of time, space, things and identity. They are words such as

All	**Always**	**Everybody**	**Everywhere**	**Anything**
Only	**Never**	**Nobody**	**Nowhere**	**Everything**

They can expand awareness and open up possibilities, or contract awareness and limit possibilities, depending on their context. When linked to a positive statement they uplift us. When linked to a negative statement they can be limiting.

<u>Positive:</u> *Everyone in this company is capable of achieving anything that they want to achieve, if they have clear purpose and determination.*

<u>Negative:</u> *Everyone in this company is useless and will never amount to anything.*

Racism, prejudice and stereotyping are often expressed in Universals, if not overtly, then by implication. All men are from Mars? All women from Venus?

A simliar generalisation occurs with classes of people such as

The managers aren't really interested in the staff's welfare.

or

The staff don't care about anything other than taking home their pay. They have no loyalty.

Implicit in those statements is *all* managers and *all* staff. We saw with fuzzy plural nouns that the language can be clarified and challenged with the questions:

Which managers/staff specifically?

and

Who specifically?

Universals rarely withstand challenge, because there is usually an exception to the rule declared by the Universal. Notice that I didn't say that Universals *never* withstand challenge. Sometimes Universals correctly state the truth. In some companies, for instance, it may be true that none of the managers is interested in the staff's welfare. But in the majority of cases you'll find that the sweeping generalisations do not hold true when challenged.

Universals can be challenged as follows:

Technique:
Challenging Universals

1 " . . . ?"

2 *Is it possible that . . . ?*

3 *Can you imagine . . . ?*

With the first technique, simply take the Universal and ask it as a question:

- We'll never be able to figure this out.
  Never?

- It's always going to be like this.
  Always?

With the first technique, it is important that you stay silent after asking the question. There will sometimes be an short period of silence during which the other person is reassessing their position, but just be patient, and await the answer.

Let's look at how to handle different responses to those two examples.

- We'll never be able to figure out the solution.

  Q: Never?

  *A: Well, maybe sometime in the future,
      but I can't see it.*

> *Q: If you could see the solution, what do you think it might look like?*
>
> *A: [describes possible solution]*
>
> *Q: How, specifically, would we do that?*

- It's always going to be like this.

  > *Q: Always?*
  >
  > *A: Maybe not always...[pause].*
  >
  > *Q: When that time comes, how would things be different?*
  >
  > *A: [gives broad description of future scenario]*
  >
  > *Q: What would you see/hear that's different?*
  >
  > *A: [describes sensory data].*
  >
  > *Q: How can we start to move things in that direction?*

Notice, how I've combined different **Powerful Questions,** and how the first answer breaks the limited (contracted awareness) belief. The questioner then works with the answer and turns it into the next question, which is designed to expand awareness and direct it towards, and emanate, a new reality. All of that can be achieved in a single question. The following question forms are useful for achieving that outcome:

> *A: Well, maybe sometime in the future, but I can't see it.*
>
> *Q: If you could see the solution, what do you think it might look like?*

and

> *A: Maybe not always...[pause].*
>
> *Q: When that time came, how would things be different?*

The new reality is strengthened with sensory-specific data that builds a capacity to 'hold' the new perspective and make it tangible and difficult to deny as a possibility.

Notice that the first quotation incorporated the visual sense, which 'paced' the phrase '*...but I can't see it.*'

The second question paced (flowed with) the time elements in 'not always', and did not refer to a sense, because no sense was mentioned in the answer.

The second and third techniques for *Challenging Universals* use our imagination to break out of the limited belief, combined with fuzzy language to postulate a scenario that is difficult to deny. Again, what those techniques do is to start the process for creating a new reality:

- None of the managers has a clue what the staff really needs to be able to perform at their best.

  Is it possible that somewhere in the company there is a manager who is more in tune with what the staff needs and who may be able to assist with this problem?

  Who specifically?

  How would you obtain their assistance?

- The unions won't agree to that condition.

  Can you imagine a scenario where the unions just might find that condition palatable, or even beneficial for their members?

  What would that scenario be like?

  How would you approach the union?

The 'If...?' question

One of the above examples used an 'If...' frame, which is a very powerful technique for expanding, directing and emanating awareness towards solutions and opportunities, and breaking out of limited mindsets.

**Technique for expanding,
directing and emanating**

If...what...?

If...how...?

If...who...?

If...where...?

If...when...?

Examples:

- *If this were possible to do,
  how would we do it?*

- *If there was an answer to the problem,
  where would we find it?*

Fudging

I anticipate	I think	I believe	I feel	Should
I expect	Likely	Possibly	Probably	Appears
Maybe	Perhaps	Could	Possible	Seems
Might	Try	Tried	Almost certainly	Intends

These, and similar, words and expressions are often used to avoid commitment or responsibility for actions or for making decisions.

The following are examples of fudging from actual reports and proposals presented to executive level (names, dates and identifying features have been changed, but the text is otherwise verbatim). Little other information was provided in the reports/ proposals to elaborate on these quotes:

- *After the initial difficulties of the first two weeks, things improved dramatically and seem to be going well.*

- *The modifications are currently being completed and will be circulated next week for further comment and should be in production by the end of September. A new form for the document will be developed when the final design is agreed. The new redesigned form is expected to be available by the end of October.*

You'll also recall the following extracts from the report that was given as an example in the *Time, Space and Measure* sub-chapter (page 115) of this book. The extracts contain quite a lot of fudging language:

- *We believe that this trend should transfer into won projects in the next four to six weeks.*

- *The client requires us to complete the final works before we receive the remainder of our claim. This should occur within three weeks.*

- *It appears that if both our clients and NatureSpan are*

successful in winning these projects we have a very busy period after the New Year break.

- *We are short listed for a number of projects that should commence shortly.*

Technique:
Turning Fudging into Commitment

1 Challenge for more certainty
   a) You think / anticipate/ believe / feel / expect ..., or it is/ you can / will / know?

   b) Likely / possibly / probably / almost certainly/ appears that.., or it is / can / will / did / was...?

   c) Maybe / perhaps / could / possible / might / try / tried..., or shall / did / didn't /will do.

2 Ask for solution
   How can we ...[improve our chances / find out the information with certainty] ?

These techniques are often linked to other **Powerful Questions** strategies .

Examples:

- I anticipate that we'll have the government's approval on that by 5th May.

   You anticipate that we'll have it or we will have it?
   How can we find out?
   How, specifically, can we gain more certainty, or speed it up?

- I think this is the best way to achieve that outcome.

    You think it is the best way, or it is the best way?

    You think it is the best way or you know it is the best way?

Then use the other **Powerful Questions** techniques to deliver an outcome:

How can we be sure/how do we know that it is

the best way?

What do you mean by the 'best' way? Compared to what?

What would you see/hear happening differently if it was the best way?

How can we improve the chances/reduce the risk?

- The unions will almost certainly support a proposition in those terms.

    Almost certainly....or will?

    Which part specifically is in doubt?

    How do we know whether they will or won't support that part?

    What are our options – how can we modify the proposal to achieve our outcome and remove the doubt for the union?

- If we continue on that path we are probably looking at a loss in the tens of millions of dollars.

    Probably? How can we determine the extent of

    financial impact?

    Tens of millions? How many tens, specifically?

- We might be able to avoid the loss.

    Might? Or will be able to?

    How can we do things so that we will make a profit on the transaction and still maintain our integrity with the customer?

- We'll try to get that done in time.

    Try? Or will?

    How do you need to do it in order to get it done in time, to budget and without causing a mutiny?

Exercise:

Challenge the Fudging language and ask for commitment in the following paragraphs

1   We anticipate that a suitable resolution might be possible provided the circumstances suit both parties.

2   It is believed that the clients will probably agree to the conditions stipulated in the draft and should be able to convince their associates to do the same.

3 Yes. I think that is an acceptable solution, one that we can probably live with. We'll certainly try to have it in place within the next week or so.

Feeling Statements

'Feeling' statements can be descriptive of intuitive responses, but in many cases they are very fuzzy ways of describing an unclear thought process. They are in a similar class of response to 'in my experience', and are best handled by ascertaining the sensory data and interpretation behind the feeling.

i) Objections and doubts – unpleasant feelings

Objections and doubts about a fact, opinion, conclusion, strategy or proposition are sometimes stated as being feelings about something – another way of saying '*I don't agree with that...*' or '*I don't want to...*' or '*That won't work*':

> *I'm not comfortable with that*
>
> *I'm uncomfortable about that approach*
>
> *That doesn't feel right to me.*

These statements are usually direct descriptions of a physical response. If asked where in the body the feeling is located, the answer is generally "*in my gut*" or "*a sensation in my head*", or "*a tension in my chest/shoulders*" etc.

The physical responses are the result of a thought or impression about the circumstances. The thought or impression is generally below conscious recognition or on the border of conscious recognition ("*I can't quite put my finger on it*") and as such can seem to be difficult to put into words.

You can attempt to deal with the unknown quantity by trial and error, but if you miss the key issue, the doubt may remain and result in dissent or conflict.

The most useful way to deal with undefined 'feeling' statements is to elicit the facts or beliefs that trigger the feeling. This is quite simple to do, but does require that you respect the deeper thought processes of the person who holds the doubt.

Technique:
Dealing with doubts/negative feelings

There are several different options.
Use one or more as appropriate to the situation.

1 *"Which part…(of the proposal/strategy)…
doesn't feel right?"*

2 *"If we did/didn't go ahead with this… (proposal)…,
what (do you think) might be the result/problem?
What would you see/hear?"*

3 *"When you have that feeling… what are the
background thoughts/beliefs about …
(the proposal)… that generate that feeling?"*

4 *"You think that…*
(choose one possible meaning at a time) e.g.

■ *the strategy might not work?*

■ *the information is flawed / insufficient?*

■ *the outcome is too uncertain?"*

Example : Eliciting the sensory data behind an objection

*I'm sorry, but I can't agree to that course of action. It just
doesn't feel right somehow.*

This statement is fuzzy. What is 'it'? The next question (below) withdraws awareness from 'feelings' and back to sensory information on which the feeling is based. This approach does not negate or deny the feeling, but simply clarifies the cause of the feeling. The feeling is a response to the way the person is thinking, perceiving and interpreting data. I have added some comments to highlight various points.

Q: Which part of the proposed course of action doesn't feel right?

A: All of it.

Q: All?

A: Yes, all. (Definite global assertion; break it down to chunks/specifics)

Q: Is there any one aspect of the proposal that is of particular concern?

A: Yes, the part on page 12 to do with implementation.

Q: What, specifically, about the implementation is of concern to you?

A: I'm not convinced that the strategy will produce the outcome that we want.

Q: If we implemented the recommended strategy, what do you think might be the result (instead)?

A: I think it is likely to meet a lot of resistance from the financial markets.

Once the sensory information is elicited, obtain specifics and find a way to improve the data, strategy or proposal so that the doubt or objection is alleviated and the person who raised the doubt is comfortable/satisfied (i.e. the feeling is reversed):

(example continues)

Q: What do you mean by resistance?

A: Lowering their recommendations. I think it would be perceived as an expensive move that is unlikely to reduce costs in the long run.

Q: How do you know that to be their perception? On what do you base that?

A: That was their response a couple of years ago when X company did something similar.

Q: Were economic conditions similar at that time?

A: Pretty much. No significant difference.

Q: What did X company do, and how can we do it differently so that the implementation strategy produces the outcome we want, and current market perception is favourable?

(Discussion of how to do that –
various options and improvements)

Q: OK. We agree that there is a better way. If we did it that way, how would you then feel about the strategy meeting the outcome and being acceptable to the market?

A: Good. I'm sure that would work.

The doubt has now been removed.

It is very, very difficult to change a feeling without changing the thought process upon which the feeling is based. It is far more useful to bring the background thoughts into the open, where they can be assessed and negotiated.

The benefit of this approach, as with all these techniques, is that they by-pass adversarial conflict and assumptions (so far as feasible) and constantly seek better ways to do things.

It will not be possible in *all* cases to satisfy an objection. If it is not feasible to find a way that overcomes objections, works, and retains general support, you may have to take a vote/consensus or agree to disagree.

ii) Enthusiasm – eliciting the sensory data behind 'good' feelings

Support for a proposition can also be expressed in terms of feelings:

That feels right to me.

I feel that we are on the right track with this strategy.

The danger with the 'good' feeling statements is that

➤ colleagues agree without understanding what they are agreeing with

➤ no (or insufficient) further options are considered

➤ warm feelings are substituted for due diligence.

Again, the feeling is a response in the body to what is often an unseen or unspoken thought or perception about the circumstances.

Problems may occur when everyone makes the same assumptions that lead to the 'good vibrations', without testing the assumptions:

That feels right to me.

Good, what about everyone else?

Yes. Feels OK to us.

OK, lets run with that.

Each person may feel good about the proposition for different reasons, based on different assumptions, one or all of which may be inadequately grounded.

Technique:
Five ways to test/challenge
the assumptions of positive feelings

1 *What specifically is it about this option that feels good?*

2 *What is the difference between this option and the other options that makes this one more acceptable?*

3 *How do we know that it will have the impact/outcome/ result that we believe it will have?*

4 *What is the objective (see/hear/feel) evidence to support that?*

5 *Is there another way that might work even better?*

Review

✓ Don't believe everything you read or hear. Most 'facts' are actually not facts. They are someone's opinion, belief or interpretation.

✓ Challenge the other person to produce source evidence in the form of sensory data – what was seen, heard, felt, smelled and tasted.

✓ Ask the question: *How do you know that (to be true/accurate)?*

✓ When making a decision based on critical data, and a lot is at stake, get the source information if possible, and verify the source. - *"How was (the evidence) obtained?"*

✓ Deal with each sense separately, starting with the most relevant sense for the data.

✓ 'Absolutes' are words that allow no exception to actions or process. They are usually used to limit behaviour and contract awareness: e.g.   Can't   Have to   Should.

✓ To challenge Absolutes ask:
  What would happen if . . . (we did/didn't) ?

✓ Universals are words that allow no exception to issues of time, space, things and identity. They are words such as:
  All   Always   Everybody   Never   Only

✓ Universals can expand awareness and open up possibilities, or contract awareness and limit possibilities, depending on their context. When linked to a positive statement they uplift us. When linked to a negative statement they can be limiting.

✓ To challenge Universals ask:

" . . . ?"; or " *Is it possible that. . . .*"

- ✓ Technique for expanding, directing and emanating:
  If...what/how/when/where...?

- ✓ Fudging words and expressions are often used to avoid commitment or responsibility for actions or for making decisions – e.g. it is anticipated, I believe, it seems.

- ✓ To turn Fudging into commitment: Challenge for more certainty and ask for a solution.

- ✓ 'Feeling' statements are usually direct descriptions of a physical response. The physical responses are the result of a thought or impression about the circumstances.

- ✓ The most useful way to deal with undefined negative 'feeling' statements is to elicit the facts or beliefs that trigger the feeling e.g.
  "Which part...(of the proposal/strategy)...doesn't feel right?"

- ✓ The danger with the 'good' feeling statements is that colleagues agree without understanding what they are agreeing with, no (or insufficient) further options are considered and warm feelings are substituted for due diligence.

- ✓ The most useful way to deal with undefined positive 'feeling' statements is to elicit the facts or beliefs that trigger the feeling e.g.
  "What specifically is it about this option that feels good?"

Practice suggestions

1 Take a few minutes to complete the exercises in this section, if you have not already done so.

2 Over the next few days:

- Practise listening to news services, talk-back radio, interviews and conversations specifically for the purpose of hearing when you could verify facts, challenge assumptions, opinions and interpretations, and challenge Universals, Absolutes and Fudging and Feeling Statements. Focus on one pattern at a time until you are comfortable with it, and formulate the appropriate question. Initially, just listen for the pattern, and when you are able to recognise the patterns easily, practise listening to the content of the discussion simultaneously with challenging the pattern.

- Practise listening to lengthy discussions, keeping track of those patterns and asking the appropriate questions to challenge them.

- Review a recent report, proposal, briefing paper or strategic document. Identify the patterns and formulate the questions to challenge those patterns. If you find any words of phrases that you'd like to clarify, call the person who presented the document and ask them the question, if appropriate.

- Review the documents for your next meeting and highlight the assumptions etc. Consider which of the marked items will be of most value to challenge, and formulate the questions you will ask initially, and any follow-up questions.

- Ask the questions in a conversational manner to maintain rapport.

5

Setting Frames

Chapter 5

SETTING FRAMES

Frames are the parameters within which the mind is directed by a question, and are powerful influencing and negotiation tools. Frames expand, contract, direct and focus awareness towards defined outcomes:

Examples:
The frames are in italics:

- How can we modify the proposal *to achieve our outcome and remove the doubt for the union.*

- How can we determine the *extent of financial impact.*

- How can we do things so that we will *make a profit on the transaction and still maintain our integrity with the customer.*

- How do we need to do it in order to *get it done in time, to budget and without causing a mutiny.*

You can add in as many parameters ("and X, and Y, but not Z") as you like – a bit like Boolean language for an internet search engine.

A change in frame will cause a different result. The art is to:
The principle is:

We can modify or change the frames to shift the outcome. The key

**Frame the question to achieve
the most useful outcome.**

to successfully framing a question is to know what outcome and parameters you want the other person to consider.

The mind flows where the question goes.

We can take the above examples and modify the questions to generate significantly different thought processes and have significantly different outcomes. When you read the original version of the questions (left column) and the modified version (right column) in the table below, observe the shifts that occur within your own awareness as the questions change. In particular, do the modifications expand, contract, direct or focus your awareness more so or less so than the original versions?

Original	Modified
How can we modify the proposal to achieve our outcome and remove the doubt for the union.	*How can we modify the proposal to achieve our outcome without having to consider the union.*
How can we determine the extent of financial impact.	*How can we determine the extent of financial impact in the next 24 hrs so that we can resolve this issue promptly. (time focus)*
How can we do things so that we will make a profit on the transaction and still maintain our integrity with the customer.	*How can we do things so that we will make a profit on the transaction (deleted further qualification relating to integrity).*
How do we need to do it in order to get it done in time, to budget and without causing a mutiny.	*How do we need to do it in order to win, period.*

Frames reflect values and ethics

Notice how values and ethics can determine the scope of the question, the answer and the actions that follow. If a Board were to put the last two questions from the right hand column to a CEO, would it be fair for the Board to complain that the CEO behaved unconscionably?

Those two questions explicitly or implicitly expanded the scope of behaviour that is acceptable.

The frames that we choose to place on our communications reflect values that are often unspoken and unrecognised.

> **Your choices reflect your values, moment by moment.**

Designing the question

It's worth taking a little time to practise designing questions which create the shifts of awareness that will obtain the result you want. Initially, you may find it easier to write the design process down, but the ultimate goal is to be able to create the question in your mind as you are participating in discussions. Once you know the formula, and with a little practice, you'll be able to shape the question as you are asking it. You won't have to formulate the entire question before you ask it.

The following steps will assist:

1   Define the outcome that you want from the question

2   Select the core form of question most appropriate to the outcome

3   Specify any conditions, parameters or frames that are to be taken into consideration in achieving the outcome

4   Use the formula:

> **Core form + outcome + frames.**

Imagine that you are in a meeting with five other colleagues discussing a problem with a manufacturing process that is a component of the product manufactured at the plant. The problem arises randomly, and when it occurs it causes damage to part of your product. That stoppage does not impact on the total plant production, and can be absorbed within the production schedule if it does not occur frequently. However, the frequency of the problem is increasing and your team has some concerns that soon the interruptions will start to interfere severely with the production schedule.

The best assessment of the problem so far is that there is a glitch in the software that controls the manufacturing process. However, no one is sure if that is the case, and your technicians have recommended that the production line be shut down for five or six hours while they attempt to identify the cause of the problem and fix it. They say it is impossible to locate and identify the source of the glitch, or to repair it, without a shutdown. That amount of down time will be very costly because it will impact the entire plant operations and delivery schedules in your company's 24/7 operation. The meeting is going around in circles and you want to focus the minds of the people in attendance on getting the problem sorted out as soon as possible.

The core form of the question: Since you will be looking for a strategy for developing and implementing a solution, the form of the question will probably be either

> *'How can we...?'*

or

> *'If there was a way... how...?'*

The outcome: Locate and fix the problem

Frames: You have several options for adding frames to the core question:

- No downtime on the specific production line on which the glitch is occurring
- Maintaining daily target output for the plant
- Minimising downtime on the production line
- Minimising the loss of daily plant output.

Initially you want to try to prevent downtime on the production line, but you will have to expand the team's awareness and take them out of the 'impossible' belief in order to do that. You will have to use a question that expands awareness significantly. The components of your question might be:

<u>Core form of the question:</u>

> If there was a way that [outcome]…and …[frame] how could it be done?

<u>The outcome:</u>

> Locate and fix the problem.

<u>Frame:</u>

> Have zero downtime on the production line.

The question would be:

> *If there was a way that we could locate and fix the problem and have zero downtime on the production line how could it be done?*

The question expands the mind beyond the current beliefs and directs and focuses the mind into a search for a new way of dealing with the problem so that there will be no downtime. If the technician's belief that it is not possible to locate and fix the problem without stopping the production line for six hours is strong, he may say:

> *It can't be done.*

You'll then apply other questions:

> *Q: Is it possible that there may be another way of doing this that we haven't thought about yet?*

A: Sure, but I don't know what that would be.

Q: I understand. But if there were another way, what do you think it might be?

Perhaps, after trying that line of questioning, no alternative strategy has been devised, so you can fall back to the next best question, simply changing the frame to allow for realistic downtime on the specific production line but maintaining overall plant production output:

If there was a way that we could locate and fix the problem, minimise downtime on the production line, and still maintain daily target output for the plant, how could it be done?

That question may trigger some innovative strategies for juggling production so as to compensate for the production line downtime.

If that is also not possible to achieve, you have another fall back position, for which a slightly different core form of question would be appropriate, together with a change in one of the frames:

How can we locate and fix the problem, minimise downtime on the production line, and minimise the loss of daily plant output?

When using frames, I recommend that you use no more than three frames in one question (in addition to the core question form), otherwise the question becomes too convoluted and loses focus. If you have more frames that you'd like to add, choose the two or three most useful frames for the initial question and then add the extra, minor frames after the answer is given:

And how could we adapt that answer to [insert extra frame e.g. ensure that we maintain delivery schedules to customers]?

When working in teams, there is considerable benefit in engaging the team to identify the outcome and frames. If you do that, it is helpful to write their responses on a flipchart and from the list on the flipchart, identify the outcome and frames that are important for the issue that you are discussing. You can ask the group:

> ➤ *What is the outcome we're looking for here?*

> ➤ *What are the conditions, parameters or frames that we need to take into consideration in achieving the outcome?*

then formulate the question accordingly. You might have to prompt the form of question if the other team members don't know the various forms available. Then put the question to the team to answer, and they'll own the question (process) and the outcome (content).

Exercise:

Phrase the single question that is most likely to deliver the desired outcome with each of the following scenarios.

1 Some of your fellow Directors/Executives want to immediately approve a proposal to purchase a small company that you all believe will add value to your business in a specific niche market. However, you and several of your colleagues are concerned that you don't have sufficient information about the certainty of the target's revenue to make a clear business decision. A vote has not yet been taken. The numbers on either side of the debate are equal, except for the undisclosed view of the Chair, who has a casting vote. Your company's competitors are positioning to make overtures for the same target. Information received suggests that offers will be made to the target by two competitors within the next few weeks. You don't want to be dragged into a bidding war if you can help it.

---

2 You have a draft strategy for improving profits that you
   believe is a winner. The Unions have traditionally objected
   to similar strategic moves.

   a) History suggests that it's best if the union does not get
      wind of the initiative until it's a *fait accompli*. The company
      can't afford for the initiative to be delayed or thwarted
      because the opportunity has only a short term window to
      get started.

   b) As above, but you want the company's employees on
      side without hindrance from the union, which has been
      impossible in the past because the union has a strong
      influence in the company.

   c) As per 2(a), but you need the union on side because the
      employees will probably hate the idea.

   d) You've just realised that the strategy has a fundamental
      flaw, and won't work. Which question do you ask?

Review

✓ Frames are the parameters within which the mind is directed by a question, and are powerful influencing and negotiation tools.

✓ Frames expand, contract, direct and focus awareness towards defined outcomes.

✓ A change in frame will cause a different result.

✓ The art is to frame the question to achieve the most useful outcome.

✓ The mind flows where the question goes.

✓ We can modify or change the frames to shift the outcome.

✓ The key to successfully framing a question is to know what outcome and parameters you want the other person to consider.

✓ Your choices reflect your values, moment by moment.

✓ Use the formula: Core form + outcome + frames.

✓ Involve your team in identifying the outcome, frames and form of question – and, of course, in answering the question if you want ownership and commitment.

Practice suggestions

1   Complete the exercise in this chapter.

2   Practice formulating the question on a past report that you have received, using the formula given in this chapter.

3   Practice formulating the question for a meeting that you will be attending in the near future, using the formula given in this chapter

6

The Ripple Effect:
Identifying Hidden Meaning,
Unstated Purpose
and Implications

THE RIPPLE EFFECT
(WHOLE-OF-SYSTEM IMPACT)

E ach proposition, strategy, solution and argument has numerous hidden layers of meaning, and impacts numerous frames of reference. The meanings and frames can give powerful insights into

> ➢ Implications for the bigger context: the impact of the proposition on the company (goals, strategy, values, vision) and whole system

and

> ➢ the proponent's personal motivation (personal goals, ambitions, desires) .

The meanings and frames are also extremely useful components to use with negotiating, influencing, consulting and consultative selling strategies.

Cascading sideways

We have already looked at techniques for cascading down to sensory-specific data using the forms of question "*What specifically do you mean by...?*", "*What did you see/hear/feel...?*" and "*How, specifically...?*" Those questions seek details, or smaller chunks of information.

'Cascading sideways expands the context, and seeks to understand the bigger picture. It considers the implications and meaning beyond the immediate considerations, like the ripples that travel out from the point where a stone is dropped into a pond – hence it is the 'ripple effect'.

The form of the question for cascading sideways is:

> *What is/would be the result/outcome/impact/effect/meaning of* [the actions or circumstances] *on/for* [frame]?

The following is a summary of the technique and some common frames:

Technique:
Identifying unstated purpose and implications

OPERATIVE QUESTIONS

1 What is/would be the result, outcome, impact, effect, meaning, ...

Examples:

What is/would be the result (for/to)...

What is/would be the outcome (for/on)...

What is/would be the impact on...

What is/would be the effect on...

What does/would that mean (for/to)...

2 Why do you want (to do) this?

FRAMES

Our / your...

Business

Revenue

Profits

Market share

People

Customers

Productivity

Reputation

Growth

Cash flow

Strategy

Cash reserves

Cash flow

Values

Vision

You.

Add other frames as appropriate to the context of the discussion

---

The basic formula for this technique is similar to the formula used for setting frames, except that 'Actions' is substituted for 'Outcome':

Operative question + Actions + Frame?

'Action' can be a decision, recommendation, proposal or other form of action.

i) Example of using the ripple effect to understand implications:

A cost cutting proposal has been submitted to you. You notice that the proposal does not say anything about risks associated with cutting the costs, but you know from what you've read in the business press over the past 10 years that cost cutting can be counter-productive if the consequences of cutting costs is not properly considered.

The form of question most commonly used for understanding implications utilises the words

- result
- outcome
- impact
- effect, or
- mean

What does/would [that action] mean...for/to...?

What is/would be the result of...for/on...?

What is/would be the outcome of...for...?

What is/would be the impact of...on...?

What is/would be the effect of...on...?

Select the operative that focuses the mind on what you want to know - the result, impact etc.

Operative: What would be the impact of ... on....?

Actions: cutting back room costs

Frame: our ability to monitor trading desk activities.

The question would be:

> *What would be the impact of cutting back room costs on our ability to monitor the trading desk activities?*

By changing the frame slightly you can shift awareness to behaviours of the traders:

> *What would be the impact of cutting back room costs on the likelihood that the traders will or will not adhere to risk disciplines?*

In the case of both those questions, the answers can be tested and improvements sought by the use of some of the other **Powerful Questions**:

> *How do we know that will be the impact?*
>
> *How can we cut the costs **and** reduce the impact and risks?*
>
> *If there was another way to reduce costs and risk in an acceptable balance, what would it be?*

ii) Example of using the ripple effect to identify an unstated purpose (personal motivation):

An unstated purpose is not necessarily a deceitful purpose. It is simply one that has not been stated openly. In many cases, that purpose will be a vague idea in the mind of the person offering the solution or strategy, or something that they consider to be only marginally relevant to the discussion, such as their personal satisfaction. However, personal satisfaction can be a powerful driver of behaviour, actions and choices in business, and may be very relevant to a decision whether or not you would approve a proposal, or approve a particular person to lead the proposal.

The questions in this technique generally elicit answers that shift awareness to the right (fuzzy, global end) of the specific/fuzzy continuum, providing a higher meaning, linked to the bigger picture. By eliciting the higher meaning you can

- tap into the motivation that is behind a seemingly ordinary request, and

- at the same time view the value system of the person who is answering the question.

Identifying an unstated purpose may provide insights into other people's (and your own) motivators and values that are useful when delegating tasks or considering career opportunities.

Example: *Recommendation: That we agree in principle to expand the business overseas and nominate a task group to draw up a strategy for overseas growth.*

The form of question most commonly used for identifying unstated purpose utilises the word 'meaning':

Operative: What would be the meaning of ... for....?

Circumstances: Expanding overseas

Frame: The employees

The question would be:

- Q: *What would be the meaning of expanding overseas for our employees?*

- A: *More security with alternative growth markets and some protection against local recession.*

- Q: *And what would more security mean to our employees?*

- A: *Less worry about whether they'll have a job or how they'll pay the mortgage or clothe their kids when our (country's) economy starts declining.*

- Q: *And what would that mean to them?*

A: *Less stress at home, happier in their job.*

Q: *What would it mean to you if we expanded overseas?[Switched frame to 'you'.]*

A: *Security for the business, the employees and me and my family, but also challenge, satisfaction, and opportunity - assuming that I play a role, which I'd like to do.*

Q: *What would challenge, satisfaction and opportunity mean to you?*

A: *I'd be able to fulfil more of what I'd like to achieve in the next 5 years.*

Q: *What specifically would you like to achieve in the next five years?*

In that example, we cascaded up through "the meaning of the meaning" to employees and then switched to the meaning for the person answering. That person's values and motivators behind the recommendation are now more transparent. Security, challenge and taking care of employees and family are now identified as being important to that person.

The answers also provide a better idea of the balance between self-centred motives and business-centred motives, which may impact on whether you will agree to that person taking a lead role in any overseas expansion.

You can ask the question several times, using two or three different frames, before asking the 'you' frame. I usually leave 'you' until last in this technique, and get the business frames out of the way first. That way, the questions have far more impact for when the 'meaning for you' or 'impact on you' is asked.

Use one frame at a time, particularly if you are cascading up, otherwise the 'meaning of the meaning' will become confusing for the listener. For instance, if you ask:

What would be the meaning of expanding overseas for our employees and for profits?

the person may answer the 'profits' or 'employees' components or attempt to answer both in one answer. That means you'll lose one answer or receive a double barrelled answer. If the latter, you'll probably have to split the answer into 'profit' element and 'employees' elements in order to ask for the next higher meaning.

Two or three frames will generally be sufficient to elicit the key motivators. Use the Pareto Principle and target the frames that have the most value. If you are the CFO, you'll want to know the impact on the company's finances. If you are General Manager, you may want to know the impact on staff morale and production. If your experience tells you that there will be a potential issue for customers or suppliers, use customer and supplier frames for the question.

Notice also how each answer leads to the next question. Each question takes it's cue from the previous answer, unless switching frames. The answer about challenge, satisfaction and opportunity generated a question about what challenge, satisfaction and opportunity would mean; the answer about achievement generated a question about what that means.

.....but also challenge, satisfaction, and opportunity .....

Q: *What would challenge, satisfaction and opportunity mean to you?*

A: *I'd be able to fulfil more of what I'd like to achieve in the next 5 years.*

Q: *What specifically would you like to achieve in the next five years?*

That is what I referred to earlier as 'staying present' with the person's answers.

However, the last question switched to a clarifying question, ("What specifically...?) so that we know what the person is talking about. We could go on and ask '*What would achieving that mean to you?*', but I'd probably choose not to go too much further in a normal business discussion (three levels of cascade up, like the three levels of specifics to sensory data, usually produces enough good quality data) because the answers become fuzzier the higher up the scale of meaning we go.

That does not mean you shouldn't go higher. Ultimately, the process will generate answers that are related to higher consciousness and life purpose, and that extent of cascading upwards may well be useful in certain circumstances such as coaching. However, some people would feel uncomfortable going that far unless an appropriate relationship (such as coach) was first established. Ensure that you have, and maintain, full rapport and trust if you take the questions higher. And respect that relationship.

At first, asking the questions may seem a little uncomfortable, because we are not used to asking this type of question in business, and secondly, because it may seem like prying into the person's mind. The question activates the person's internal process of consciousness, and elicits their personal meaning of the circumstances, even if the question is about the company's profits etc. However, it is a very beneficial question, because it expands awareness and provides a larger context for decisions and behaviours that may otherwise not be recognised or understood.

This technique is extremely useful for helping people with local initiatives to understand, and take account of, the impact of their proposal on other parts of the business:

What would be the impact on your internal customers?

and for management to understand and take account of the impact of their decision on local work areas:

What would be the impact on staff in that area if we undertook this change initiative?

followed by other **Powerful Questions** such as:

How do we know that?

How can we find out?

How can we implement or modify the initiative so that the potential problems are reduced or eliminated?

Cascading up

Instead of shifting 'sideways' to morale, profits and other topics, you can cascade 'vertically' by asking for 'the result of the result'. That is done by using the answer to the previous question as the action in the formula:

e.g. If I spend more than I earn, I'll run out of cash.

> **Operative question + Prior answer + Frame**

Q: If you ran out of cash, what would be the impact on your finances?
A: The result of that is I'd have to borrow more, or sell assets.
Q: If you had to borrow, or sell assests, what would be the result?
A: The result of that is that I'd owe a lot, own nothing and probably be bankrupt in a year or so.

Upward cascades are a very useful tool in business. I use them in our Vision, Values and Strategy workshops with executive teams and throughout their companies to step up (expand) the levels of awareness necessary to generate a powerful Vision and integrate (hold) cultural change initiatives across all aspects of the business. We also use upward cascades to create impact when coaching, to ensure that the client makes a clear choice to leave behind (withdraw, disengage) those behaviours, actions and strategies that don't work and to embed (hold) the choices that *will* work.

The questions are excellent for use in consultation, for 'solution' or 'consultative' selling, and for negotiations and mediation. The following are examples of how the questions can be used

(i) in negotiations/sales and

(ii) to verify the viability of a proposal where the proposer has not considered the full implications and is relying on inadequate data.

Example:
Handling an objection based on personal values

Two parties are negotiating for the sale/purchase of a business.

Business owner:

The terms are not acceptable. It wouldn't work for us.

Q: *If you did accept the terms, which I understand you don't want to do, what would that mean for your company? [ripple question]*

A: *We'd lose many long term employees in the merger, people who rely on us to put bread on the table, and who are like family to us.*

Q: *And the outcome of that for you? [upward cascade]*

A: *I'd retire wealthy but with an uncomfortable conscience.*

Q: *If we can work out a way that you'd be comfortable with in conscience, would you consider the matter further?*

Combining different forms of questions

Example:
Impact not considered

Strategy Z for a major new HRIT project, costing $10 million, has been proposed by the HR Department. That amount is well above the year's IT budget. The IT department's suggestion is, instead, for strategy Y to be approved.

CEO:

Q: *Why do you want to do Y as opposed to Z?*

A: *It is the best way. We have to get this fixed or we'll have significant problems with meeting revenue projections for this year and each year thereafter until it is fixed.*

Q: *So you believe that Y is better than Z?*

A: *Yes.*

Q: *In what way, specifically do you believe that Y is better than Z?*

A: *It is a quicker way, and less expensive. [This answer relates to speed and cost, omitting reference to impact on people].*

Q: *What effect do you think Y would have on staff? [ripple question, switched frame to consider staff]*

A: *I don't believe it will affect them substantially. [fudging]*

Q: *How can you be sure of that?*

A: *My project manager has looked at that and she is satisfied that it won't have a big impact.*

Q: *What did she say?*

A: *That there doesn't seem to be any great concern among staff about the impact.*

Q: *Specifically, as best you can recall, in quotes.*

A: *She said "I asked my team to check with the staff affected by this option as to what they thought about it. The staff could not see any problem."*

Q: *Do you know how many staff were asked, what information they were given about the consequences and the strategy, and what it would involve for them?*

A: *Not specifically. I'm sure that they were given a proper briefing. The project manager is very competent.*

The CEO may well want to ask for better quality information on this issue.

You'll probably have noticed that I have used a number of the **Powerful Questions** patterns in that last example. The questions can be used in any combination that works for the outcome you want.

Review

✓ Each proposition, strategy, solution and argument has numerous hidden layers of meaning, and impacts numerous frames of reference.

✓ The meanings and frames can give powerful insights into the proponent's personal motivation and context - the impact of the proposition on the company.

✓ The meanings and frames are also extremely useful components of negotiating, influencing, consulting and consultative selling strategies.

✓ Cascading sideways and up seeks to understand the bigger context.

✓ The form of the question is:

What is/would be the result/outcome/impact/effect/meaning of [the actions or circumstances, or previous answer] on/for [frame]?

✓ An unstated purpose is not necessarily a deceitful purpose. It is simply one that has not been stated openly.

✓ The questions in this technique generally elicit answers that shift awareness to the right (fuzzy, global end) of the specific/ fuzzy continuum, providing a higher meaning, linked to the bigger picture.

✓ By eliciting the higher meaning you can tap into the motivation that is behind a seemingly ordinary request, and at the same time view the value system of the person who is answering the question.

✓ Identifying an unstated purpose may provide insights into other people's (and your own) motivators and values that are useful when delegating tasks or considering career opportunities.

✓ Ultimately, the process will generate answers that are related to higher consciousness and life purpose. That extent of cascading upwards may well be useful in certain circumstances such as coaching.

✓ Ensure that you have, and maintain, full rapport and trust if you take the questions higher, and respect that relationship.

✓ The question activates the person's internal process of consciousness, and elicits their personal meaning of the circumstances, even if the question is about the company's profits etc.

✓ 'Cascading up' is a very beneficial question, because it expands awareness and provides a larger context for decisions and behaviours that may otherwise not be recognised or understood.

✓ This technique is extremely useful for helping people with local initiatives to understand, and take account of, the impact of their proposal on other parts of the business, and for management to understand and take account of the impact of their decision on local work areas.

Practice suggestions

1   Listen to conversations, interviews and talk-back radio. Whenever a course of action is recommended or proposed, formulate an appropriate upward cascade question.

2   Practise formulating the upward cascade question on a past report that you have received, using the formula given in this chapter. Do the exercise for both motivation and implications.

3   Practise formulating the question for a meeting that you will be attending in the near future, using the formula given in this chapter. Imagine the possible answers and take the cascade up three levels, then switch frames two or three times, finishing with 'you' (to three levels). Do the exercise for both motivation and implications.

4   In your next meeting, ask 'cascade up' questions once to level 2 for both motivation and implications (in relation to different points). In your next coaching situation, ask a cascade up question to level 3 for both motivation and implications.

Handling
Disagreement, Criticism
and Negativity

Chapter 7

HANDLING DISAGREEMENT, CRITICISM AND NEGATIVITY

D isagreements and conflict are based on different 'shapes of consciousness':

- perceptions of facts
- interpretations of facts
- experiences
- opinions
- assumptions
- beliefs.

The majority of disagreements and conflicts in business can be readily facilitated to a workable and productive outcome with the *Powerful Questions*.

Disagreement provides an excellent opportunity to test and probe for better facts, opportunities and solutions, and to understand different perspectives about an issue.

The problem occurs when disagreement is taken as a personal affront, or becomes a technique for personal attack, but even then the *Powerful Questions* will be a very useful tool.

I was asked to do an interesting job recently. A division of a large heavy engineering company was being hampered by serious tensions between management and sections of staff. The Divisional Manager had received death threats from staff. The tensions resulted in a direct cost to operations of close to $1million per annum. The Regional General Manager (RGM) of the organization asked me to mediate an initial meeting of the warring parties and if possible work towards finding a solution. I requested a 4-hour morning session to deal with the issue, plus lunch to be provided for the participants after the session.

The RGM initially hesitated about arranging lunch. He did not believe that it was possible for the parties to be cooperating, and to want to have lunch together, after only one session of 4 hours, because of the difficult history of the conflict.

The two most senior Divisional Managers and three staff/union representatives attended the facilitated meeting. I applied the **Powerful Questions** first to clarify and test current positions and facts, then gave the group a short exercise that enabled them to understand how they applied the processes of consciousness to create the conflict, and how they had the power to change those processes to let go of the conflict.

After a mid-morning break, the participants were invited to (individually and separately on flipcharts) answer eight **Powerful Questions**. When that was done the participants shared their answers. They immediately realised that they all really wanted the same outcomes, but were in conflict over the strategies for the outcomes.

I then asked further combinations of the **Powerful Questions** to facilitate the group to alternative strategies that worked for each of them and their stakeholders.

When the RGM arrived for lunch, he was surprised to see and hear all parties enthusiastically and amicably discussing when and where to next meet to implement their solutions.

That was volatile situation, but it is illustrative of the effectiveness of the questions. Most disagreements are much more civil, but are nevertheless based on the differences mentioned above.

There will always be differences of opinion and perception in any business. If not, then you'll want to check to see if the people in the business (and the company itself) are still breathing. Disagreement is not something to be afraid of, or to avoid. It can be a healthy way of testing ideas and opening doors to better solutions, strategies and opportunities. In business, the objective is to find and do what works. You'll find that easier to do if the parties leave their egos at the meeting room door, as the saying goes. Take the attitude *"Maybe the other person has a point. Let's explore and see whether they might in fact be right or have a better solution. Maybe there's a way of improving both our ideas."* If their point does not stack up to scrutiny, you'll be more certain that you've made a sound business decision. If their point does stack up, you'll have found a better way to achieve the outcome.

That approach is what we call the Aikido method of doing business. Aikido is a martial art in which you use the energy of the other person to immobilise them. The harder they attack, the faster and easier it is to defeat them. Basically, you 'go with their flow', moving in the same direction as the attacker and then turning their energy back towards them.

The situation is similar with the questioning formats, except that you don't turn the answers against the other person, but re-direct them towards a useful outcome. You still, however, 'go with' the person's answers in the manner described earlier – staying present and forming the next question from each answer.

The basic technique for handling disagreements draws on the various **Powerful Questions** outlined in this book. One of the reasons we call them 'powerful' questions is that they can be adapted and blended in various combinations to apply to many business situations, once they are understood and practised.

Technique:
Handling Disagreement

1   Clarify what the other person disagrees with

2   Obtain specific information about the other person's views, beliefs, opinions and 'facts', their evidence and their higher intention and desired outcome

3   Modify *your* idea/view and/or insert your opinion, evidence and higher intention and desired outcome

4   Explore 'how specifically' to achieve any common purpose with a mixture of yours and the other person's ideas, or a completely different solution or to obtain more evidence

5   Agree actions and responsibilities that suit both parties, or agree to disagree.

Handling Disagreement - sample questions
Add more questions as appropriate to the circumstances

1   Clarify what the other person disagrees with:

What, specifically, don't you agree with?

Which part, specifically, don't you think will work?

Which specific part of the data don't you believe?

For stategies, solutions, processess:

Which part do you disagree with?

If the answer is "I disagree with all of it!", go through each section individually and ask: "*What about this part?*"

2 Obtain specific information about the other person's views, beliefs, opinions and 'facts', their evidence and their higher purpose:

   What is your view on that issue?

   What do you think would work better?

   What do you believe to be the correct data?

   What do you believe would be the outcome?

   What outcome are you looking for?

   ...and the result of that?

   How do you know that to be a fact?

      - What are the facts on which you base that view?

      - Did you see/hear/feel/experience it?

      - What specifically did you see/hear/feel/experience?

      - How did you conduct your research?

- What is/would be the meaning /impact/outcome/result if I am correct?... How do you know that?... If you are correct?...How do you know that?

3 Modify your idea/view and/or insert your opinion, evidence and higher intention/desired outcome:

> *I disagree with your opinions in the following aspects...*

> *Specifically, I do not agree with...*

> *The facts on which I base that, and my own view, are...*

> *I researched the matter in the following way...*

> *I disagree with the outcomes you suggest for your/my view as follows...I believe that the outcomes of your /my views are as follows...My view is based on...*

> *However, I agree with what you said about X, and I'm happy to modify my views as follows...*

> *or*

> *I hadn't considered that. I think it is a fair point, but I think we need to change one aspect of your approach....*

or confirm your view and insert your opinion, evidence, and higher purpose:

> *I understand your data. I don't agree with your inference from the data, because ....(state your reason/alternative evidence).*

4 Explore 'how specifically' to achieve any common intention with a mixture of yours and the other person's ideas, or to obtain more evidence.

The common ground is based on answers to the Ripple Effect questions (both sideways and upwards) in steps 2 & 3.

What are we both really trying to achieve here?

Where do we have common ground/agreement?

How can we do this in a way that meets both our outcomes?

Your way doesn't work for me, my way doesn't work for you - what's another way we can achieve the outcomes that we are both looking for, ways that will work for both of us? How can we modify or combine or change those ways to get an even better solution?

5 Agree action and responsibilities which suit both parties, or agree to disagree.

So we agree to do X [be specific and get feedback]?
We agree responsibilities as follows [be specific and get feedback]?

or

We don't agree on X. Can we agree to obtain better data so that we know which position is correct?
We don't agree on Y. Can we agree to disagree and find another way to move forward?...How, specifically, can we move forward? If there was a way around this issue, what would it be?

Reframing personal criticism and abuse

This technique is not appropriate when someone simply says "I disagree" or "I don't think that's a good idea", in which case you can use the *Handling Disagreement* technique. The Reframe technique applies to more extreme forms of disagreement when you receive negative personal comments about what you have done or said, or when your ideas, decisions or actions are the subject of those comments.

e.g.

You don't know what you're talking about.   *You're an idiot.*

That's a stupid idea.   *That's an unworkable idea.*   *Rubbish!*

The technique for reframing personal criticism and abuse has been one of the most popular processes in our programs for many years. I designed this technique to counter the 'audience from hell' that I encountered early in my public speaking career. In fact, it was my first big speaking engagement, and nearly my last. It was at a business conference and some of the audience had a bit too much to drink and became somewhat belligerent and unpleasant by the time my speaking spot arrived. I made the mistake of reflecting what they were saying in an attempt to clarify their meaning, which only dug the hole deeper. So I did my 'lawyer' thing and went on the attack as nicely as I could. I eventually managed to bring the event back to where it should have been, and the troublemakers left the building, but I was not satisfied with what I did, and looked for a better way.

Since discovering the reframing technique outlined below, I've never 'choked' when subjected to criticism or been 'out of power' on the stage or in meetings if any negativity is occurring. The reframing technique enables you to stay in your own state of balanced power in any situation. The key is to memorise the questions in the first step so that the appropriate question runs off your tongue automatically as soon as you hear the criticism.

233

Technique:
Reframing personal criticism and abuse

1 State the fact.

Choose one of the following questions:

You don't...

> ***agree*** *with what I said?*
> ***think*** *it will work (that way)?*
> ***believe*** *the data?*
> ***agree with*** *the data?*

(Then run the 5 Step 'Handling Disagreement' technique), i.e.

2 Clarify what the other person disagrees with

3 Obtain specific information about the other person's views, beliefs, opinions and 'facts', their evidence and their higher intention

4 Modify your idea/view and/or insert your opinion, evidence and higher intention

5 Explore 'how specifically' to achieve any common intention with a mixture of yours and the other person's ideas, or to obtain more evidence

6 Agree actions and responsibilities which suit both parties or agree to disagree.

The first step (the reframe) switches the attack back to the attacker. Then it is simply a matter of applying the '*Handling Disagreement*' technique after Step 1. Thankfully, you'll usually only need to go to Step 2 or 3 in the Reframing technique before the other person realises that they don't have the facts to sustain their criticism. Most abusive criticism is not well founded, and that generally becomes evident by Step 3. My only word of caution is this: when the tide turns in your favour, don't go for their jugular and humiliate the other person. Look for a way to save their face if possible, and build a solution and outcome that works, and a relationship that works. You may have to do business with that person in future.

Example:

Abuse:	*You must be stupid. That's the dumbest thing I've heard in a long while.*
Reframe Question:	*You don't agree with what I said?*
	A: No.
Disagreement model:	*Q: What, specifically, don't you agree with?*

or

Reframe Question:	*You don't think it will work?*
	A: No.
Disagreement model:	*Q: Which part, specifically, do you think won't work?*

or

Reframe Question:	*You don't believe/agree with the data?*
	A: No.
Disagreement model:	*Q: Which part of the data, specifically, don't you believe/agree with?*

Then proceed with the remainder of the disagreement technique.

Generally the form of criticism and the topic of discussion will provide clues as to which Reframe question is likely to be most appropriate. If you have been providing data and the criticism is aimed at your data, then the Reframe *"You don't agree with the data?"* is most relevant. If you have stated an opinion, then the Reframe *"You don't agree with what I said?"* is applicable. When the criticism is about a strategy, the Reframe *"You don't think it will work?"* is the best choice.

However, if you are not sure which form to ask, use two of the forms:

> *You don't agree with what I said or you don't agree with the data?*

The person will then choose one or the other (or both) or provide some other basis for their comments. Similarly, if you select one of those questions and the other person does not think it is applicable, they will usually correct you:

Q: *You don't think it will work?*

A: *No, it's not that. It will probably work. I just don't think it is the best strategy.*

Remember, if you receive that answer, you have a Comparator to clarify ('best'). There are two issues – what part of your strategy do they believe is not the best, how do they know that, and could they improve that strategy; and which strategy do they believe is better, how would they do it, and how do they know it will work?

As a memory aid, always start the Reframe with '*You don't...*', and memorise the four options in Step 1. The words '*You don't...?*' place the responsibility and focus for the issue on the person who has the issue, instead of on you. As soon as they answer 'Yes...', they have taken back ownership of the problem that they have with what you said in your presentation.

'Yes' means 'Yes, I don't agree, I don't believe, I don't think it will work'. In other words, the question focuses the person internally on their own reality, instead of externally on you. Once they have switched internal, clarify their reality further until you understand what they are thinking that leads them to disagree. It is the Aikido principle again.

When you understand their perspective, it is fairly easy to insert your perspective:

> *I understand what you are saying, but I disagree on the third point. Your tests may state that X, but we conducted tests using a slightly different, but more reliable, method, and the results were Y. That's why we disagree.*

So, it's no longer a matter of you being stupid, but rather that you have conducted tests using different methods and there is a difference in results. The criticism is much easier to deal with from that perspective, and if you have an audience, you'll probably come out the winner.

Review

✓ Disagreements and conflict are based on different 'shapes of consciousness': perceptions of facts, interpretations of facts, experiences, opinions, assumptions, beliefs.

✓ Disagreement provides an excellent opportunity to test and probe for better facts, opportunities and solutions, and to understand different perspectives about an issue.

✓ There will always be differences of opinion and perception in any business. If not, then you'll want to check to see if the people in the business (and the company itself) are still breathing.

✓ Disagreement is not something to be afraid of, or to avoid. It can be a healthy way of testing ideas and opening doors to better solutions, strategies and opportunities.

✓ In business, the objective is to find and do what works. You'll find that easier to do if the parties leave their egos at the meeting room door. Take the attitude *"Maybe the other person has a point. Let's explore and see whether they might in fact be right or have a better solution. Maybe there's a way of improving both our ideas."*

✓ The techniques in this section are similar to Aikido. Basically, you 'go with the flow', moving in the same direction as the attacker and then turning their energy back on them. The situation is similar with the questioning formats, except that you don't turn the answers against the other person, but re-direct them towards a useful outcome.

✓ The **Powerful Questions** can be adapted and blended in various combinations to apply to many business situations, once they are understood and practised.

✓ The Reframe technique applies when you receive negative personal comments about what you have done or said, or when your ideas, decisions or actions are the subject of those comments.

✓ The reframing technique enables you to stay in your own state of balanced power in any situation.

✓ The key is to memorise the questions in the first step so that the appropriate question runs off your tongue automatically as soon as you hear the criticism.

✓ The first step (the reframe) switches the attack back to the attacker. Then it is simply a matter of applying the *'Handling Disagreement'* technique after Step 1.

✓ Look for a way to help the other person 'save face' if possible, and build a solution and outcome that works, and a relationship that works. You may have to do business with that person in future.

✓ To Reframe personal criticism and abuse choose one of the following questions:

> *You don't...agree with what I said? ...think it will work (that way)? ...believe/agree with the data?*

Then run the 5-Step *'Handling Disagreement'* technique.

✓ The Reframe question focuses the person internally on their own reality, instead of externally on you. Once they have switched internal, stay with clarifying their reality until you understand what they are thinking that leads them to disagree.

Practice suggestions

Handling disagreement

1   Memorise the *5-Step Process for Handling Disagreement*, and familiarise yourself with the typical questions used in that technique.

2   Ask a colleague to partner you in practising the process. Find an issue on which you genuinely disagree (preferably a business matter, but any matter will do). Give your opinion or viewpoint. Your partner then states his or her disagreement without providing details. You apply the questions and *5-Step Process* to resolve the disagreement.

3   When you next disagree with someone in a conversation or discussion, apply the technique. You may find it easier to do that initially in a phone conversation when you can have the *5-Step Process* in front of you.

Reframing criticism and abuse

There is no option but to memorise this pattern. When you need to use it, you will not have time to think or to pull out the book. The most important parts to memorize are steps 1 and 2.

240

8

Your Choice

YOUR CHOICE

To ask or not to ask, that is the question...

You must decide whether you are satisfied with what is presented to you or whether you ought to probe deeper and wider by asking more questions.

No-one is an island. What you ask or don't ask will have an impact. Ask yourself some questions:

- Do I have enough information?

- Do I understand what is going on here?

- Do I understand the implications?

- Are the risks clear to me?

- Does this proposal/information feel right to me?

- Even if it feels OK, how sure am I that it is correct/the best option?

- How can I fill the gaps so that I can be satisfied?

- If in a year's time this issue comes unstuck and I have to explain myself to investors or a court, what standard will they expect of me. What questions might provide me with the appropriate information? What action would they expect of me. Is my *not* asking an option for them?

- If this was my money at stake, what would I do?

- What would a good business leader do?

- What standard of business leader do I want to be?

- Who will look after the stakeholders?

- What is the courageous and right thing to do right now?

- What values are important for me to live by right now?

Generally you will find suitable information after you've asked two or three well-placed questions. You can then decide whether to continue further with the questions.

Do not 'back off' because of peer pressure or perceived peer pressure from colleagues. You are on the Board/executive/management team because of your values, vision, experience, expertise and ability to make good decisions. What you may lack in knowledge or experience you can make up by asking the questions that matter.

There is an old adage: *A stitch in time saves nine.* A single question now may prevent a disaster later.

It costs only a few seconds of time, or a few minutes at most, to ask the questions that may make a difference.

Practising Listening and Questioning Skills

The questions described in this book are equally applicable to the spoken and the written word. .

Obviously you, the reader, will have applied the questions to the written word in the examples that I have included in the book. You can at any time read an exercise again and analyse it in more detail. You can do the same with any written report or proposal that lands on your desk. However, you will not have that same opportunity in conversations. The spoken word does not have solid form, and is fleeting. You do not have much time to think before you hear the next phrase. That is a listening skill, and is essential if you are to apply the *Powerful Questions* to conversations, and not just to the written word.

There are many opportunities every day at work and home to practise the listening skill for *Powerful Questions*. However, if you want to learn quickly and effectively how to apply the *Powerful Questions* to conversations and documents, or to increase your skill level using the *Powerful Questions*, you will find one or more of the following options to be of benefit:

➢ Web-based learning modules where you can practise at your own pace

➢ Free blog that discuss various techniques and any updates on the techniques outlined in this book, plus associated topics of interest.

➢ Web seminars and teleclasses

➢ Coaching (one-on-one, group, telephone or internet)

➢ Master Classes presented in your company (ideal for boards, executive teams, senior management)

Please go to our web site *www.spandah.com* for more information on these options.

Accredited Trainer opportunities

If you are a coach, trainer, consultant or facilitator and are interested in becoming accredited to train your company or clients in the *Powerful Questions* skills, please contact us via *www. spandah.com.*

about the author

Christo Norden-Powers is Director of Business Development for Spandah Pty Ltd, an Australian-based consultancy that specialises in organisational transformation and change. Christo is a former trial lawyer who developed an interest in human and corporate performance, and in 1984 coached 15 Australian Olympic athletes, including medallists Gary Honey and Debbie Flintoff-King, in how to generate and maintain peak performance states. His work then quickly spread to the corporate world.

In the late 1980's Christo and a team of colleagues designed and implemented one of the largest corporate culture change initiatives in the southern hemisphere, in a $10Billion corporation. They trained over 14,000 people in a hands-on change process that ultimately led Christo, in the early 90's, to develop Spandah's powerful business communication tool, the *MasterProcess*™, a corporate culture transformation process known as the *Change MasterProcess*™, and *Powerful Questions*™, all of which are delivered to organisations in Australia and the U.K.

Christo's current and past clients include Telstra (Australian Telecom), TNT, Shell, Kellogg's, Murdoch Magazines, Ernst & Young, Australian Taxation Office, Selleys, Esprit, Coca-Cola Amatil, State Rail Authority, B & Q (UK), Metropolitan Police (UK),Frigite, Institute of Executive Coaching, Australian Institute of Company Directors, Australia Post, Reckitt & Colman, FDS (UK), State Revenue Office, Canon, Chartered Secretaries Australia.

Christo is the author of the book:
Awakening the Spirit of the Corporation (available at www.spandah. com).

He is a sought-after speaker, executive coach, cultural change consultant and governance consultant. Christo lives in Australia and works internationally.

www.ingramcontent.com/pod-product-compliance
Lightning Source LLC
Chambersburg PA
CBHW061150220326
41599CB00025B/4429